I hand over my entrance form to a young but tough-looking official.

'First time in China?'

'Yes.'

'Push green button.'

The front of the desk has four buttons lighting up. Two green, two red. The first green one says 'very satisfied' and has a picture of a very happy face. The second says 'satisfied' with a slightly less ecstatic, but still moderately content smiley face. The third button is red. It reads 'not satisfied' and the face looks somewhat downbeat. The last option is a miserable-looking 'very dissatisfied'.

Above the range of smilies is a question: 'How satisfied are you with the welcome you received in Beijing?'

'Eh ... I'll be teaching at a ...'

'Push green button!'

I push the green button, the one with the smiliest face of all. And that's that. I'm in. No doubt there'll be a news story at the end of the year claiming 99% of tourists are delighted with the reception they get in China. There is no fifth option saying 'airport is nice, but do something about the spitting'.

About the Author

Gary Finnegan is an award-winning journalist and former magazine editor currently living and working in Beijing. He has been a contributor and columnist to Irish newspapers and magazines, as well as making regular appearances on national and local radio and television including Newstalk, *The Last Word* on Today FM, TV3's *Ireland AM* and *The Late Late Show*. This is his first book.

Beijing for Beginners

An Irishman in the People's Republic

Gary Finnegan

The Liffey Press

Published by
The Liffey Press
Ashbrook House, 10 Main Street
Raheny, Dublin 5, Ireland
www.theliffeypress.com

A catalogue record of this book is
available from the British Library.

ISBN 978-1-905785-44-5

Printed in the Republic of Ireland by Colour Books.

Contents

Acknowledgements

Thanks to everyone I have met during my time in China, especially the people of Beijing. Thanks to Allison Hines for help with photos. A special word of appreciation for my friend and agent Juliana Adelman whose hard work and talent I was fortunate enough to benefit from.

For Liz,
of course

1

'Hello Big Nose'

The old man's jaw drops open to reveal seven decades of dental neglect. He's wiry and weather-beaten but has a glint in his eye. 'Da bizi!' he says as a smile spreads across his tightly-stretched face. He's sitting behind a rotting plywood shop counter on a battered stool wearing a stained vest and craning his neck to look up at me.

There's a waft of freshly smoked cigarettes mixing with the probably permanent whiff of unflushed toilets. Maybe my new septuagenarian pal had been lighting his farts on fire before I waltzed in unannounced. That would explain why he's smiling. The shop sells phone cards, cigarettes and a selection of dried fish snacks – or at least it would be if there were any customers. It seems like business is slow, even for a residential district in the less glamorous quarter of west Beijing.

I've arrived at this tiny establishment quite deliberately, but it seems certain I've been led astray. All I want is an internet cafe where I can check my email but the first place I found in my guidebook appears to have been closed down and I've spent the bones of an hour wandering around this grey old neighbourhood asking for directions. Notwithstanding the language barrier, I can't help but suspect that the locals are deliberately sending me on a wild goose chase for their own amusement. Maybe they'll meet later for a lamb kebab and a laugh at my expense.

'Did you see that lanky foreigner looking for a cyber cafe today?'

'Yeah, I had him running round in circles all afternoon. I even sent him to old man Ju's tobacco store! That oul' fella never even heard of the internet!'

The old shopkeeper's grin broadens as he repeats 'da bizi'. I haven't a clue what he's talking about so I fire ahead with the opening line of the conversation I've been rehearsing while doing laps of the locality.

'Hi, eh, ni hao (hello),' I say clumsily as I pull a Post-it from my pocket full of scribbled vocabulary notes. 'Yin te wang?' I ask, more in hope than expectation. 'Yin te wang' means internet in Mandarin and, if this chap knows the script, he'll politely inform me of the price and sit me down at a computer. Any deviation and I'll be lost.

Alas, he hasn't a clue what I've just tried to say. My Chinese vocabulary is limited to about twenty words and my mangled pronunciation usually renders these meaningless or worse. Mandarin is a tonal language, so words can have any one of four unrelated meanings depending on which tone you use. On top of that, meaning can vary wildly depending on context, giving some words over a dozen possible interpretations.

I repeat my request for the internet in other tones but the elderly proprietor is beginning to look perplexed. He's still pleased to see me though, judging by his bright-eyed smile.

'Yin' can also mean gum; 'te' can mean unusual; and 'wang' can mean elf. There are scores of combinations of these three words depending on tone and context. Hopefully he doesn't think I'm calling him a weird gummy elf. If that is what he's hearing, he's taking it very well.

It's a clammy, smoggy evening in Beijing and I'm wondering whether checking my email is really all that important. I'm still suffering a little jet-lag and a lot of culture shock. The old man beckons a young teenager who appears through grubby plastic drapes at the back of the shop. I'm ready to give up and go rather than embarrass myself by attempting to speak Chinese again.

The kid doesn't look like he belongs here. The shop is small and run down but the teenage assistant is wearing jeans and a fake Nike t-shirt, as well as a new-looking head set. He has invested serious time and effort in his hairstyle, and paid a few bob for the new Samsung camera phone hanging around his neck. Maybe he's just back from a day at the call centre doing a job that was out-sourced from Europe or the US.

The gummy old geezer gestures towards the youngster who appears to be urging me to follow him through the plastic drapes into the darkened room from whence he came. I'm hesitant but what's the worst that could happen? I suppose there could be a backstreet surgeon behind the curtain sharpening his scalpel wait-ing to remove my vital organs. But hopefully the teenager is sim-ply leading me to a local map or an older sibling with a smattering of English.

The senior and junior members of staff make an unlikely pair of co-workers so I'm presuming they are family, separated by at least a couple of generations. As I head for the drapes, I'm con-templating how easily they relate to one another and whether this might be a microcosm of modern China: the empty, dilapidated shop run by a man who is effectively retired, working with a hip, energetic youngster obsessed with gadgets and brand names. They currently coexist in perfect harmony but soon the young modern face of China will mature and the old ways will be dead. It's at once sad and exciting. I'm teasing out this highfalutin thought just to take my mind off the fact that I'm stepping into a dark unknown space and nobody knows where I am. Here goes.

A whole new world opens up as I nod a nervous farewell to the old man, who now has his trousers pulled up to his knees in a bid to keep cool. That's the last I'll see of him.

The confident teenager leads me down a short, dark corridor which opens into a dimly lit room. All I can see are sixty young Chinese men, their faces illuminated by the blue hue of their computer screens, tapping away furiously at their keyboards. It looks like the nerve centre of a subversive youth movement. That sort of carry on is frowned upon here so hopefully this is just the internet cafe I've been so irrationally desperate to find.

I scan the screens of the army of computer geeks as I walk past in pursuit of the teenager who is taking me to the only vacant computer in the room. Everybody is playing online video games, ranging from shoot-em-up bloodfests to onscreen dance practice. These dance games usually demand the player to rehearse their steps on an electronic mat but there's a whole row of lads sitting perfectly still, going through the virtual motions in the comfort of plush leather chairs. I can hardly imagine anything more innocuous. It rules out my Subversive Youth Movement theory and the Crack Squad of Government Computer Hackers hypothesis which had been building in my mind. China had been in the news the previous day for alleged cyber espionage where it was claimed that the Chinese had separately hacked into sensitive computer files held by the US, Germany and Britain. That may well be going on in an underground den down the road, but this place appears to be no more than a cyber cafe. It's almost disappointing.

My computer is the only one with a couch rather than a chair and the teenager who led me here logs himself out before giving me a password. It seems he has given up his own machine for me. I do my best to thank him with my poorly pronounced Chinese and he strolls away to make fresh tea.

The computer is brand new, state-of-the-art and comes with a headset and webcam. I'd have gratefully accepted a souped-up Commodore 64 if it had internet access, so this is way beyond the expectations I had when I walked in the door. With sixty machines on all day, operated non-stop by guys between sixteen and twenty-six, this little techie hideaway gets pretty hot and a little smelly. I'm not helping. Having walked around in the dead heat all afternoon, I'm producing at least my fair share of odour. My back is already beginning to stick to the leather sofa so I'll check my mail and be on my way. After all that, my inbox holds nothing outside of the anticipated 'Hope you're settling in' message from my family, a few good luck messages from friends and some spam.

Having recently quit a job that used to have me inundated with emails and phone messages, I'm still adjusting to the fact that checking my mail isn't really a matter of life and death. Of course, it never was, but it'll take a few weeks to regain perspective.

While I'm here, I may as well look up that word the old shopkeeper kept repeating: 'Da bizi'. I had guessed it might have been the equivalent of 'welcome' or maybe even 'we're closed'. It turns out that 'da bizi' means 'big nose'. That's right, big nose.

I've never considered myself to have a remarkable nose but it seemed to draw the attention of the toothless wonder in the shop. I read on. 'Da bizi' refers not to the size of the snout but to the high bridge of the European nose. There seems to be some debate as to whether this term is meant to be derogatory. The Chinese aren't exactly blind to racial difference but they tend to treat foreigners with respect rather than contempt. Big nose can be used as an insult but it seems unlikely that the old shopkeeper was being racist. He just hadn't seen a westerner in a while and that was the first thing he blurted out. If I inadvertently called him a weird gummy elf, he probably forgave me on the same basis.

Before I arrived in Beijing I had visions of a cosmopolitan city packed with skyscrapers and glitzy department stores. All of that can be found in the central and eastern districts of town. But I live on the west side. Out here, it's possible to go for a week without seeing another foreigner. This makes me stand out a little, and explains why people have been staring at me everywhere I go. The novelty is already wearing off all the attention I've been getting.

For one thing, it's hard to suss people out when they are looking at you. How can I stare at them when they are staring at me? It also makes it difficult to pick your nose in peace.

Plenty of people have been offering an exuberant 'hello' when I pass. I didn't mind playing the celebrity at the beginning, but once the first fifteen minutes of fame are up it gets old.

I continue reading up online about Chinese attitudes to foreigners. Overall, it's pretty positive. For example, they refer to America as 'Mei Guo' which means beautiful country. And they have a hard-earned reputation for going out of their way to make a good impression on foreign guests. However, I come across a couple of references to how Chinese people get a kick out of shouting 'hello' at gormless tourists who return the greeting with even greater gusto. This cracks them up, for some reason. I'll be holding back on the gusto on my way home.

I've run out of things to look up online so, having had one last look at my favourite news sites to check whether the West has gone into meltdown since I left, I log out and approach the cash register. One thing I was sure to learn before I got here was the numbers. So when the teenager who had earlier brought me from the shop to the cyber cafe asks for 'san kuai', I know he wants three yuan. Yuan is the formal name of the Chinese currency, but just about everybody refers to it as 'kuai' which is a bit like saying 'quid'. €1 buys about ten kuai. My bill for surfing the internet for the bones of an hour is the equivalent of 30 cent. I hand over a twenty kuai note which is worth roughly €2 and there is a minor drama as the till doesn't have enough cash to give me change. It's quickly sorted out and I leave by a side door which lands me on a narrow bustling side street.

I almost get hit by a bicycle as I scan around to get my bearings. This isn't the door I came in, but it looks no more like an internet cafe than the other side where I met the old man who first called me big nose. I wonder if it's deliberately disguised as a tobacconist and whether the old man's shop is just a front. Are there really dried fish in those packets?

There has been a clampdown on internet cafes in China in recent years for several reasons. For starters, a fire killing two dozen students in 2002 first brought unwelcome attention to the cafes. Looking at all those overworked computers in a poorly ventilated and cramped space, it's easy to imagine the same happening here. On top of that, the government has been getting increasingly worried about the amount of time young people are spending online. Illegal games, gambling and pornography are fanning the flames and several cafes have been closed for failing to prevent under 18s from using the internet. And that's saying nothing about those crazy dance-step games.

There have even been state-sponsored rehab programmes for students who spend too much time online at the expense of their studies. You'd be forgiven for suspecting that China would prefer to see the internet's power harnessed solely for e-commerce rather than free speech. The fact that blogs have been closed and several foreign websites blocked due to their controversial content would back this up. So while the number of cyber cafes and wi-fi hotspots are exploding across the globe, the nation developing faster than almost any other is cutting back.

It has gotten dark while I was inside but there's a blue and white subway sign glowing in the distance. I can walk home from here once I know what direction to take and the subway is my landmark. As I head for my new home, I'm wondering how on earth they manage to make any money in the internet cafe and why they don't increase their prices. I'm not complaining, but charging 30 cent an hour doesn't seem like it would cover the costs of buying, maintaining and powering all those new computers. In any case, demand is clearly high and competition is low. They haven't fully got their heads around capitalism in the communist alleyways of west Beijing.

The question of whether China is a communist country in name alone is one I hope to have answered by spending time here. The Chinese Communist Party is still the only political show in town but Beijing is touted as the seat of the next superpower. It seems to have embraced the global market more than any other nation and its ability to manufacture and export vast quantities of cheap consumer goods have given it a trade surplus with the US of $120 billion a year. They are better capitalists than the Americans but China has no interest in becoming the land of the free. For how long can they juggle free market economics while curtailing political freedoms?

I wasn't about to solve that conundrum, but in any case, my thoughts were interrupted by the overwhelming intake of smog that had just sent my lungs into shock. I'm coughing so much it hurts. A low smog cloud hangs over Beijing, obscuring buildings just 100 yards away. Despite the heat, I haven't seen the sun all day. China boasts sixteen of the world's top twenty most polluted cities and Beijing's air is among the filthiest on the planet. It's chronic today. I feel like I've been walking behind a bus for a week. This had been on my mind when I was online but I read that today is officially a 'blue day', according to the government. The fact that Beijing is a smoggy city hasn't come as a total shock but nothing prepares you for a day like today. Apparently there are around 200 blue days a year, which I had taken as a promise of clear blue skies for more than half the year. If this grey day is officially blue, I'm not sure how well I'll get on here. My big nose is stuffed with soot and smoke and I can feel my throat constricting. It's like the early stages of a cold but nobody else seems the least bit bothered.

I cross the main junction to the university where I'm staying, barely avoiding an old man on a three-wheeler laden down with recyclable rubbish. Proportionately, snails carry less weight behind them than this droopy-eyed tri-cyclist who labours as he slowly pushes himself and his cargo uphill. Tightly packed cardboard and flattened plastic bottles account for much of his load. These can all be sold for a small price to recycling plants. This explains why twice today, as I staved off dehydration by knocking back a lukewarm bottle of metallic mineral water, my bottle was snatched from my hand as soon as I'd finished. Who says China isn't environmentally conscious?

The old cyclist may have been moving at a snail's pace but his speed was constant. Most importantly, as far as I'm concerned, it was obvious there was no way he would be slowing or stopping if I got in his way. I only saw him at the last minute because he was travelling the wrong way down a cycle lane and I was naively watching for traffic moving in the prescribed direction.

Crossing the road in Beijing is an art, but it's probably best to think of it as a war game. Just act like everybody else on the road is out to get you. Your own paranoia is your only ally. Don't presume that cars and bikes will come at you from the directions suggested by road markings. There are no rules. This is war. Cars, buses, bikes, trucks – expect them all to emerge from the most surprising directions at the most unlikely angles. The green man is not your friend. He's a cheap hussy flashing a bit of leg, enticing you to let your guard down for the split second it will take for you to be flattened by a moped. Even when it looks like pedestrians have got right of way, cars turning right are getting the same signal at the same time. That's when it turns into a giant game of chicken, and it's when you should remember that drivers in China fancy their chances in a head-on collision with pedestrians. They plant their foot on the accelerator and their hand on the horn simultaneously to give you half a chance to retreat. At best, the green man is a suggestion that you might consider making a run for it. But be sure to look left, right, behind you, in front of you, and maybe upwards, as you sprint towards the kerb.

I survive today but promise not to become complacent tomorrow.

I'm staying in a dormitory for international students at the university where I'll be teaching next month. They're promising to sort me out with an apartment but for now, I'm in what I imagine cells in minimum security prisons look like. I've got a washroom which doubles as a toilet and a shower cubicle. This means the toilet, the mirror and, if you're as naive as I was this morning, your towels get saturated every time you have a shower. There's a drain in the middle of the floor which collects some, but not all, of the shower water. The floor is at a slight incline which encourages puddles to gather in the dark corner behind the toilet. Spirit levels must be too expensive to bother with here. It's far from ideal but at least it's relatively clean.

What really gets me is the bed. It's just a slab of hard wood on a steel frame topped off with the thinnest layer of blue-covered foam imaginable. Even when you cover it with a thick towel it's still pretty miserable. Culture shock plus jetlag and my sore throat are adding up to ensure that I can't sleep. Maybe I'd have better luck on a mattress. I'm sure this bed will leave me bruised in the morning.

As I lie in wide-eyed agony on my prison bed, I'm reflecting on my first impressions of Beijing. It's unbearably smoggy and often filthy; crossing the road is a daily hazard; I can't understand a word that is spoken or written; and my bed is as comfortable as sleeping in a bottle bank.

Why did I come here again? Will the long-term gain eclipse my short-term pain? Is China a place I want to call home for the next year? This is an analysis I probably should have run through before I boarded the plane, but better late than never.

I had started telling friends about my plan to quit work and head east months before I'd booked flights or committed to a job. I had plenty of time to sort out precisely what I hoped to get out of the experience. But when friends, family and colleagues asked the obvious questions: Why China? Why Beijing? Why now? I usually brushed it off. 'Why not?' or 'anything to get away from the desk' became standard devices for ducking the question.

In truth, I wanted to know whether I could survive in an alien culture, and China feels about as alien as it could get right now. Beijing is in line to be the centre of the universe for the next couple of decades so I may as well figure it out now rather than wait for my job to be outsourced to China.

But more than that, I wanted to feel like a citizen of the world; like I'm not confined to living in the country where I was born. Surely globalisation has delivered an era where we can survive and prosper in any developed city without much trouble. We're all the same now aren't we?

I've never felt more out of place than I do tonight. Maybe if I get some sleep I'll feel ready to battle the culture shock in the morning. I empty my suitcase onto the bed and spread my clothes out as an extra layer of protection from the rock hard wood beneath. I knew things would be different here but I hadn't expected to be using five pairs of boxer shorts wrapped in a t-shirt as a pillow.

I fall asleep stroking my nose from bridge to tip. It's not *that* big.

2

One Child Spits All

Aportly woman spits on the pavement as she shuffles past the steps outside the university dorm, missing my foot by half an inch. I'm wearing sandals and the thought of slimy saliva between my toes is decidedly unappealing at this time of the morning. It's 10.00 am and I haven't had breakfast, but judging by what she just spewed out, I'd guess this rotund lady has recently eaten a spring roll. There are a few traces of pastry flakes suspended in her spittle.

I stop and stare at the spitter but she hasn't even raised her head. Spitting is routine in China. It's not helping me bridge the culture gap but perhaps I'll be used to it in a few days. Is habitual public spitting really something I want to adapt to? Aren't there some aspects of foreign cultures that are just plain disgusting?

At the risk of acting like a spoiled foreigner, I can't see any merit in teaching the next generation of Chinese to spit just like their forefathers did.

I'm feeling neither open-minded nor tolerant this morning.

The sound of people hacking up thick phlegmy spits was one of the first things that greeted me as I walked across the tarmac at Beijing International Airport. Staff on the runway were taking turns to clear their throats and deposit viscous saliva on the apron.

'Thank you. Welcome to China,' chirped the cabin crew as we entered the terminal building. Surely there's a minister for tourism who could discourage spitting at the airport? It doesn't make the greatest first impression. The Beijing authorities are very concerned about what foreigners think about them but I didn't quite get the chance to share my suggestion for an airport spitting ban.

I had been put through the ringer at the Chinese Embassy at home when trying to sort out my visa. By the time I'd got the results of my medical check-up and letters from my new employer inviting me to work in Beijing, I had just four days to process my visa application. That transpired to be cutting it fine and I eventually got my passport back the day before I was due to fly out.

Aggravating matters further, the embassy managed to mistakenly give me a one-month tourist visa instead of a twelve-month working permit. This induced cold sweat from me and heated exchanges behind the visa-issuing desk. By the way she hung her head after the altercation it looked like the junior clerk was getting the blame.

While I waited for the correct visa to be pasted into my passport, I observed a series of disputes between embassy staff and wannabe tourists. Anybody banking on a two-day turnaround time was told to forget about it – it takes almost a week to issue visas – and several people were flatly informed that they would have to change their travel plans. There were tears and pleading but the embassy staff never budged one inch. The take-home point was that the Chinese authorities are not to be trifled with.

With the visa fiasco fresh in my mind, I was a little wound up about getting through passport control at the airport. All foreign passengers had already filled out two detailed health and security forms on the plane. They just want to know for sure that you're not a spy or a walking flu pandemic waiting to happen.

I had solemnly guaranteed that I did not have 'any reading material that might be detrimental to the Chinese State'; nor was I packing any transmitters or recording devices; or hosting any infectious diseases. Whatever the chances of getting bird flu patients to bring quarantine upon themselves, I doubt too many foreign spies own up before they even get through customs. They are trained for that kind of thing.

'What went wrong with the mission, 009?'

'Sorry sir, I fell for that bloody "are you a spy" questionnaire again.'

Arriving at the passport control desk with forms in hand, I'm irrationally concerned that they'll want to single me out for interrogation. On my visa application I'd declared myself to be a teacher even though that won't strictly be true for another couple of weeks. In truth, I had been working as a journalist until last week. They don't like journalists around these parts.

I've never seen so many unsmiling uniformed officials. There's not much banter between the staff. This must be serious stuff. I join a swiftly-moving queue where a stern woman is collecting the health declaration forms. She stacks them in an orderly pile without even glancing at the answers. Maybe they sift through them at the end of the day, but probably not. I bet they sell them to a recycling plant.

Then there's another form to fill. I have to inform the authorities of my new address and all the places I plan to visit. I'd been warned not to mention Tibet because that can lead to lengthy interrogations to make sure you're not a bloody human rights activist or a fan of that dastardly peace lover, the Dalai Lama.

I've no firm travel plans but wouldn't rule out a trip to the vast Tibetan plains. Still, it's best not to overcomplicate things, so I say I'm just going to work in Beijing and holiday in Shanghai. I'm really uptight at this stage and keen to fill all requisite questionnaires and get this over with. But all the pens have been stolen. A Brazilian couple lend me theirs and I quickly complete the final form.

One of the uniformed men is barking orders. I don't know what he's saying but I know he means it. He seems to be insisting that we move to another queue. We do what we're told. He tells us to move down one more, then immediately changes his mind and asks us to move back. This guy's toying with us.

The queue moves with surprising efficiency. Okay, I'm up. There's probably nothing to worry about. I hand over my entrance form to a young but tough-looking official.

'First time in China?'

'Yes.'

'Push green button.'

The front of the desk has four buttons lighting up. Two green, two red. The first green one says 'very satisfied' and has a picture of a very happy face. The second says 'satisfied' with a slightly less ecstatic, but still moderately content smiley face. The third button is red. It reads 'not satisfied' and the face looks somewhat downbeat. The last option is a miserable-looking 'very dissatisfied'.

Above the range of smilies is a question: 'How satisfied are you with the welcome you received in Beijing?'

'Eh ... I'll be teaching at a ...'

'Push green button!'

I push the green button; the one with the smiliest face of all. And that's that. I'm in. No doubt there'll be a news story at the end of the year claiming 99% of tourists are delighted with the reception they get in China. There is no fifth option saying 'airport is nice, but do something about the spitting'.

I stroll through, relieved but still convinced that there must be another checkpoint. And there is – customs. But it's as rigorous as the health and passport inspections. Another uniformed man collects my written declaration that I have nothing to declare and offers a kind smile-and-nod combination. I'm feeling upbeat while waiting for my luggage, until a Chinese man on the opposite side of the conveyor belt clears his throat. Surely he's not going to spit, not indoors. Indeed he does and nobody bats an eyelid, except for the four blonde American girls next to me who can't believe their eyes and ears. I'm seeing a pattern here.

Still a little stunned by the woman who had greeted me with a morning spit, I resolve to put it to the back of my mind and head for the park opposite the university campus. I puff out my cheeks, step over her spittle and prepare to take on the traffic. It's not as smoggy as yesterday but breathing is no longer an unconscious process. I'm thinking of all the tiny carbon dust particles passing through my nose, down my throat and into my lungs. My throat is lined with mucous today, presumably as a reaction to the on-slaught of smog yesterday. I'm tempted to vigorously clear my throat and hack it up on the path but I'm not ready to go native just yet.

Cars and bikes are whizzing past as usual, but I outwit the lot of them by slipping into the underground station and popping up at the exit on the opposite side of the road: another small personal victory against my motorised aggressors.

I'm shocked to find there's an entrance fee to what looks like a public park. All the locals are wearing identity cards around their necks, granting them free entry, but it'll cost me 10 kuai. Maybe they are learning how to be greedy capitalists after all.

They're all out today, young and old. In fact, the very young and the very old seem to be over-represented. It's mid-morning and there appear to be plenty of grandparents minding their children's children. A fit looking woman in her sixties walks past with a three year old in tow. Granny is twisting her upper body 90° to the left, then to the right, as she walks. Everybody seems to be here to keep fit. Another woman walks briskly past swinging her arms like aeroplane propellers.

And there's an outdoor gym. It looks like a playground for grownups. Everything is covered in thick coats of plasticised paint

– primary colours only. Old people are doing sit-ups and swinging from bars. They are working the cross-trainer and grappling with the climbing frame. It's all fairly unsophisticated machinery. There are no heart rate monitors, or calorie-burn counters; no hyperactive fitness instructors or wall-mounted flat screen TVs. But it is free and the locals have bought into it. Cancel your €600 gym subscription and fly to China.

Even apart from the geriatric playground, we're all here for exercise. Except for me, of course – I'm just here for a nose around. There are men walking backwards; women beating their stomach and thighs as they chat to their neighbours. Nobody has come to the park to sit under a tree and eat ice-cream. There's a high octane game of table tennis between a pair of retirees. This pair aren't messing around. There are some quality rallies and they're not shy about contesting every point. Ping pong is effectively a national sport in China.

Even the people on benches are not sitting still. They are twisting their bodies and moving their arms. Some people are having a good long stare at me. I tell myself it's probably because I'm a big-nosed foreigner, but they might be gawping in disgust because I'm the only person in the park who's lazing on the grass staring at the locals.

A happy young couple look on proudly as their son plays with his grandfather. Another couple are engaged in a three-way game of what I've always known as 'donkey' but they probably call something else. There's another content family out for a stroll with their son. And a man walking purposefully with his six-year-old boy, each of them carrying a badminton racquet.

The cutest little girl I've seen all day skips past with her mother. Pigtails, frilly dress, wide eyes – delighted with herself. Hang on. She's cute by any standard, but is it partly because she's among the only little girls I've seen all day? I have another quick 360° scan around me. There are no large families here this morning and small boys are definitely in the majority. The penny drops. The gender imbalance is a by-product of China's One Child Policy. Known in China as the Planned Birth Policy, the 1979 rule was brought in amidst fears that there simply wouldn't be enough food to feed the masses. It remains the grandest population control experiment in human history and is regularly attacked by western human rights campaigners. However, the Chinese see it as a fact of life.

'Hello!' shout three girls almost in unison, turning their heads away sharply as soon as I move to respond. They find great amusement in the greeting but recoil into a mortified huddle when I veer in their direction, retracting their necks like frightened tortoises.

The most confident of the three struggles for composure and speaks again from behind her hand. She has a long straight fringe which hangs over a single strip of thick hair forming a wide 'm' shape across her brow. 'We are sorry for disturbing you,' she squeaks, while her accomplices continue to titter. I compliment her on her English and suddenly she assumes an air of confidence that seemed most unlikely thirty seconds ago.

'You are American?'

'No, I'm from ...'

'You are English! Are you tourist?'

'I'm not English and I'm not a tourist. I'll be teaching at the university ...'

Cue uproarious laughter accompanied by a display of more wonky teeth than ought to be crammed into just three mouths. All three are ecology students from Guangdong Province who have come to Beijing early to get settled at the university ahead of the first semester, and all three are fiercely excited to meet a foreigner.

The ringleader is bordering on cocky at this point and does most of the talking while her sidekicks supply supportive nods and vocabulary as required. They interview me in depth until I've thoroughly detailed where I come from, what I think of the neighbourhood and, of course, why I chose to relocate to Beijing. I still don't have much of an answer to the last question. 'I want to get some teaching experience,' I say. That's a lie.

When they exhaust their bank of questions, I turn the tables and find they are as unimpressed by Beijing's air quality as I am. Their hometowns, I'm assured, are much cleaner and must be visited. I make an empty promise to take a trip to Guangdong by the year end.

This is the first time any of them have left their province even though they are about to become postgraduate students. They have already finished their bachelor's degrees, which would make them around twenty-two. Between the giggles and their cutesy Hello Kitty backpacks, I'd have had them pegged as fourteen-year-olds.

As I try to wind up the conversation, the chatty one – who wants to be called Kathy – suggests we all go to a bar they found last night. It's just gone 11.30 am.

'It's a bit early to drink alcohol and I haven't eaten yet today.'

'Noodle bar! A noodle bar!'

Silly me, I should have known. There isn't anything remotely resembling a pub in my new neighbourhood, despite the high concentration of students. It's all teahouses and quickie restaurants.

We exit by a gate at the far side of the park and I follow the whispering girls to a tiny, low grade restaurant. They hold one another's hands in a chain as we ramble. The students' demeanour is not what you expect from PhD researchers who are supposed to be the next generation of innovation and independent thinking. The extended adolescence enjoyed by academically successful Chinese students continues until their late twenties when they expect to finish college. At that point, there's a desperate scramble to bag a spouse and have a child.

The girls bark orders at the half-dead waiter in the noodle bar who returns a frighteningly short time later with four bowls of spicy beef noodle soup with fried eggs floating on top. It's fast food, Chinese style. The restaurant is filled with tightly-packed tables and chairs that screech and scratch the tiled floor with every movement. Identically compact eateries line these streets offering more or less the same range of noodles and rice dishes. The restaurants look suitably designed for the most populous nation on the planet. The aim is to feed as many people as possible, as quickly as possible. Product diversity is not part of Beijing's version of capitalism. If you don't like noodles you're in the wrong town.

After some agonising small talk, I ask Kathy whether she is the first in her family to go to university. She looks at the ponytailed girl to her left, whose translation draws a perplexed frown from Kathy.

'You mean do I have siblings in College? I don't have siblings – I'm from a big city!'

Families living in cities are allowed just one child, whereas those in the countryside can have more. Suddenly, there's an opening to talk about China's population control policy. Matters of social and political import are generally taboo but I'm still pretty green so I go for it.

'Of course. Forgive me. How do you feel about not having any brothers and sisters? How many children would you like to have yourselves?'

Silence. Three bespectacled heads are buried in their bowls, intensely slurping noodles. I've crossed a line. Now would be a good time to change the subject.

'Seriously though, what do you make of it? Would you change it? Do people complain about it privately?'

Still no joy. After sixty awkward seconds, Kathy drops the little girl act and adopts a more assured but discrete tone. 'Maybe it's not ideal but it is the best for China. We are 1.3 billion people and many are very poor. If we had more people, there would be starvation and the poverty.'

The ponytailed girl, who prefers to be called Luna, pipes up: 'But the rule will relax when we have children. If two people who have no siblings get married, they can have two babies. It stops the One, Two, Four crisis.'

They were slow to get into it but once they warm up, it's all chat. Luna describes how the shifting demographics have put a heavy burden on her generation. With life spans on the up, this generation of twenty somethings are saddled with two parents and four grandparents to support, hence the 'One, Two, Four'.

Bright sparks like these are expected to finish their education and repay the family by funding their parents' retirement. That was all very well when the Chinese lived into their early fifties but these days life expectancy is seventy-three. An only child has nowhere to spread the cost of supporting older generations so the authorities in Beijing are relaxing the rule to allow two adults from the first 'one-child' generation to have two children.

There are other exceptions. Ethnic minorities are allowed to have more than one child and Chinese couples returning from overseas are also exempt. The third student, a tiny girl with 'Wish You Happy Everyday' written in bubble writing on her pink t-shirt, mutters something through her braces about twins and triplets. Kathy elaborates, explaining that having multiple births from a single pregnancy does not break the planned birth policy. This is a loophole often exploited with a little help from fertility technology – it's an incentive to have twins.

Back in 1979 when China's reforming leader Deng Xiaoping introduced the rule, IVF was in its infancy. These days, it presents

Beijing's elite with the reproductive equivalent of a two-for-the-price-of-one offer.

My science-savvy lunch mates point up another major technological change: pre-implantation genetic diagnosis – a fancy new IVF technology allowing doctors to look at an embryo's genes before placing it in the womb. In practice, this means families who want boys can discard female embryos, thus contributing to China's startling gender imbalance. But, pragmatic to the last, the use of fertility science for sex selection is seen as an improvement on the cruder methods of gender discrimination still practiced in rural areas.

'Baby girls are aborted and abandoned,' whispers Luna, looking around self-consciously. Chatting to a foreigner about such sensitive issues is not exactly encouraged and the strain of wanting to make a good impression without being unpatriotic is beginning to show.

I'm putting the students in an awkward position but Luna has hit on something I've been curious about: Why do Chinese families favour boys so heavily and what does it mean for society?

Despite their porous vocabulary, between them, the girls do their best to boil down a complex cultural issue to a single point. Asian families have always preferred boys because sons work the land. Sons inherit the family plot which is passed down though the generations. Daughters, on the other hand, are traditionally seen as having joined their husband's family after they marry.

In the days when couples had five and six children, there was almost always at least one son, and daughters were easily married off to a local boy. Sons inherited farms; daughters married young farmers. Everything worked out. That is, until an artificial stress was thrown into the mix by the government. And what happens when you've only got one toss of the genetic coin that could bear you either a son or a daughter? People try to fiddle the odds. 50:50 is just too risky.

Millions of girls have been aborted, abandoned or neglected. This is why boys outnumber girls at birth. It's why infant mortality is higher in females. It explains the decline in the female population during childhood. And ultimately results in millions of single men with no hope of marriage.

For every 100 girls in China, there are 117 boys. Even if 100% of the girls find a mate, there are still 17 lonely bachelors with nobody to dance with at the disco. This might go some way to explaining the exponential growth in prostitution over the past decade. Demand for female company could hardly be higher.

By 2020, there will be 30 million more men than women in China. The prospect of having 30 million frustrated young males who face fierce competition for wives, jobs and depressing studio apartments is giving rise to fears of social instability. 'Bare branches' is the despairing label used to describe the unpaired adult men for whom marriage is not an option. These are limbs of the family tree with no offshoots.

With good wives – or any wives – so hard to find, a game of social snakes and ladders is afoot.

The girls fold up in hysterics when I suggest that young women are in a position to do a little social climbing, whereas men have nowhere to slide but down. This means some women will probably 'marry up', bagging men who might otherwise be out of their league.

Luna thinks I'm horribly cynical when I ask whether wily families are strategically switching their preference from sons to daughters in the interest of social ascension. She shoots me down with a flatly delivered rebuke: 'People get married for love in our country,' as if to suggest that the Chinese are not concerned with something as vulgar as money. 'Anyway, a girl joins her husband's family after marriage so her parents will not make money if their son-in-law is rich,' adds Kathy. It sounds like she has already thought this one through.

The natural losers in this lopsided love match are men in the lower socioeconomic classes. Dystopian visions of marauding crime gangs venting their pent-up frustration on society are exercising the minds of China's leaders. Indeed, China's neighbours are a little uneasy about the prospect of the Chinese dragon's burgeoning human firepower. Historians warn that nations with an excess of men who have no meaningful stake in society have a habit of building great armies for terrible wars. India's preference for boys means it too will have millions of bare branches – maybe they could arrange a futile bloodbath as a population control measure. China lays claim to a chunk of Kashmir. That usually gets Indians hotter than Rogan Jhosh. Pencil the Asian War in for 2025.

Other Asian countries like South Korea and Vietnam also show a strong preference for sons, although their gender ratio is not as skewed as China or India.

Even Chinese villages with otherwise rudimentary health services have access to ultrasound. 'Officials can find women hiding babies in their wombs,' explains Luna with monotonic matter-of-factness.

Putting a figure on the number of backstreet abortions is impossible, but the millions of baby girls in Chinese orphanages is evidence enough that girls simply are not of equal value to many Chinese parents.

I continue to ask whether there is any clamour to have the law changed, but the girls continue to say it's not an issue. The only people who seem concerned by it are meddling foreigners. Here, the biggest complaint is that the rule is applied inconsistently by Chinese Communist Party officials.

For the good of China, young people are happy to have small families but it's a little galling to see the rich openly flout the law because the punishment is relatively small. The primary tool for keeping parents in line comes in the form of financial penalties.

We're talking fines here, not just the cost of shoes, childcare and Spiderman merchandise.

Fines are based on the offenders' income and those in breach of the policy are often denied bonuses at work – great news for scabby bosses. But a second child is also denied access to education grants and its parents are stripped of their right to free healthcare. This forces them to pay medical costs for the entire family, not just for the newest arrival. It's an approach that works for ordinary people of meagre means, but is no deterrent to the wealthy.

However, central government in Beijing has a new stick up their sleeve to hit them where it hurts. In particular, they are targeting rural officials who have a reputation in some provinces of ruthlessly enforcing the law from nine-to-five, before returning home to their own large families. These are the kind of communists that reckon they are more equal than others.

Beijing realises that reining in these corrupt local kingpins is crucial to maintaining harmony in the countryside. But fines haven't done the trick. Even if the financial penalties were doubled for defiant officials, it would only double the hardship for local peasants. Fat cat Party cronies, working hundreds of miles from Beijing, can simply impose their own tax on desperately poor locals to help pay their own pesky fines. So Beijing hopes to tarnish their precious reputations.

Bigwigs who ignore the population control policies will be named, shamed and taken down a social peg or two. They will be barred from holding public office or receiving awards, and the lofty status they enjoy will be diminished.

'This is an excellent policy by the Politburo,' says Kathy. I agree and decide against arguing that it was Beijing that created and buttressed the countryside's corrupt CCP officials in the first place. So I ask whether they think the policy has been a success. Indeed they do and they've got the figures to prove it.

'In the 1950s, families had at least five children. Now the average birth rate is 1.75,' Kathy argues, in a way that suggests she's the star of her college debating team. On a point of information, the birth rate was down to below three kids per family when the policy was introduced so it can't be the only reason for the reduction. Birth rates fall as countries develop. But again, I'm out for information rather than an argument so I let that slide. In any case, Kathy's on a roll and she won't be interrupted.

'The People's Republic of China has always worked to contain the demand for food and resources and it is not time to end the policy, despite our great economic success.' Given the enthusiastic nods of the other girls, I take it that Kathy has correctly presented the official line.

It's true that there has been some form of population control for at least sixty years. Long before the one-child policy was officially born, there were public information campaigns designed to make small families the social norm. 'One is good, two is okay, three is too many,' went the slogan. If I can get my hands on one of these old posters, I might stick it up next to the biscuit tin – keep the cholesterol in check.

Another handy slogan, 'late, long, few', urged couples to delay starting a family and have a small number of well-spaced pregnancies. This happens to be the kind of pattern that emerges naturally in developed countries, leaving some governments worried that people are leaving it too late to have children. Indeed, even without taking drastic measures, China would probably have slowly reined in its soaring population growth over time, just as India has.

'Are there *any* downsides to the policy?' I ask.

'Yes, but there will be new measures to solve this,' says Luna, in a tone that suggests they are getting bored and suspicious of my persistent interest in this topic.

The problem, they say, is selfishness – hardly an ideal communist attribute. Authorities are worried about the impact of having an entire generation of urban adults who grew up without siblings. The social and economic gulf between life in China's industrious cities and the flagging countryside has only been widened by the population controls. Wages in big cities are already around three times higher than in the country. So there are one-child families in the city with enough money to spoil their only offspring and still live relatively comfortable lives, while country folk have one-third the income and twice the number of children.

But will these spoiled city brats – or Little Emperors, as the Chinese call them – have the cooperation, communication and social skills to thrive in the workplace? Having been lavished with attention and generally gotten their own way since they were born, these kids could be a most annoying generation of adults. Luna says colleges encourage teamwork and communication skills to help make sure it doesn't become a problem.

The conversation has become increasingly stilted as the diner fills up for the lunchtime rush so I decide not to grill my reluctant interviewees any further. In any case, we finished eating ten minutes ago and should make way for new punters.

I'm still thinking in Euro so I ignore the students' protests and happily pay the €2 bill and bid them farewell. Paying for lunch makes me feel less guilty about nosily bleeding them for information. I thank the three smilers for their company and squeeze out the door.

I wave my ticket at the man sleeping behind the ticket desk at the entrance to the park and head for home. The park is still full of grannies and grandsons, busy whiling away a summer's day. I'm looking at half a dozen spare branches and wondering what's in store for them. They are right to come here to keep fit; it gives them a better chance of wooing a wife when the time comes. Any

27

four-year-old sitting at home playing computer games will regret his lazy complacency later.

While I've been daydreaming, lots more lively little girls have been enjoying the sunshine with their grandparents. Lucky things. Even the ugly ones will land themselves a grateful suitor.

'I suppose I should get my hair done and splash out on a new dress for the dance on Saturday night.'

'Why bother? Market forces mean we're in demand. You'd score wearing clogs and a black sack.'

A pair of twin girls comes around the corner wearing twin dresses and holding what look like twin ice-pops. Maybe the gender see-saw isn't as visibly imbalanced as it seemed when I first scoped out the playground.

On closer inspection, those aren't ice-pops, they're meat sticks. A popular treat for kids here is processed meat on a stick. It's like a vertical skewered hotdog, served cold. I've yet to try one.

Given that the One Child Policy doesn't apply to multiple births, I wonder whether these twins are the product of IVF. And if so, should I be pleasantly surprised that doctors didn't discard these female embryos when they were in the dish? I'd like answers to these questions but decide against quizzing the twins on account of the language barrier amongst other things. I'll have to look elsewhere for answers.

Just then a Little Emperor spits on a duck that has been innocently swimming around all morning avoiding paddleboats in a small pond. The mini monarch lured the duck in with a lump of bread and gobbed in its face. Brat. The Emperor's father spits out whatever he was chewing and saunters over smiling.

Imagine being the father of a cocky male toddler who spits in public. I'm welling up with vicarious pride.

3

Jobs for the Boys

Security guards are everywhere in Beijing. But with ages ranging from fourteen to nineteen and not the promise of a facial hair between them, they're not exactly an intimidating force.

They guard everything from supermarkets to garden gates. In many cases, the oversized uniforms are supplied by employers, but the task of finding suitable footwear falls to the low-income teenage sentries. This explains why so many of them choose to match their dark green trousers with scruffy white running shoes. I don't suppose they care too much for high style.

'Wow, Han Ying, those vintage 1997 faux Adidas plimsoll's go smashing with your bottle green pants. And the burnt orange tee you've plumped for under your standard issue pastel green chemise really sets the whole thing off.'

They love to wear uniforms in Beijing but they aren't so fussy about fashion.

This adolescent army should not be confused with the police or the official military. The latter are not to be messed with. But the omnipresent squad of guards are just kids who need jobs, protecting things that are under no real threat.

Outside the university, a five foot six baby-faced watchman stands on a box. It lends him a certain air of authority, and makes him almost as tall as the average villain. It's not that I want students or teachers to be in danger, but I wouldn't mind if we came under attack just once so we could see how the guard would respond. Did his afternoon's training include hand-to-hand combat or did it focus on standing straight and uniform maintenance?

Across the street at the supermarket, there's a lazy-looking guy leaning against the doorframe in a navy blue suit with a badge sewn onto the side of his shoulder. He's meant to be giving off an air of authority but hasn't been doing a great job. He doesn't seem to care that there are pirate DVDs for sale two feet from the entrance, siphoning punters who might otherwise buy the real thing inside.

The guard outside McDonald's next door stares straight ahead while unlicensed food stalls undercut the chicken nuggets on sale through the golden arches. What would it take for him to spring into action? The Hamburglar, perhaps.

Let's face it, these lads are doing jobs that don't exist. In China, underemployment is preferred to unemployment.

Through the door of the supermarket I can see a group of three female employees having a good old natter. Two of them are linking arms and leaning into one another rather than stand on their own two feet. Such camaraderie. Such redundancy.

I'll venture in presently, but first I'm earnestly rifling through the fake DVDs outside. I had been eagerly anticipating having ready access to cheap pirated blockbusters. Maybe this is why I came to China? It's not the most satisfying of answers to the question of what motivated my move to the East, but it's the best I've come up with so far. If nothing else, the steady flow of foreign films into China helps attenuate the culture shock. Now if I could just find a bucket of popcorn I'd be set.

About three billion DVDs are sold here every year but at least ninety per cent are counterfeit. The Beijing side-street video store is the scourge of Hollywood. This is partly why the US has been harping on at China about enforcing intellectual property law. And while I know it's wrong for poor people in developing countries to enjoy cheap entertainment because it stands in the way of rich Californian film studios getting richer, I'm still going to support this dreadful black market by snapping up a few bargains. Honestly, I feel terrible.

There must be hundreds of titles on offer. They have copies of films that have barely been showing a wet week in the US and have yet to grace European cinema screens. Quality can vary, I'm told, but it's so cheap you can't go far wrong. There's a clear leaning towards big name stars like Cruise and Jolie, and action movies dominate over drama or comedy. It's all new releases; old movies have been dumped or recycled. I pick up a copy of *Babel* starring Brad Pitt and Kate Blanchett and read the blurb. It's predominantly in Chinese except for one large bold English pull-out quote on the back.

It reads: 'Well-meaning twaddle.'

The review is taken from that bastion of art criticism, the *Atlanta Journal-Constitution*. It's refreshing in a way. There are too many over-hyped films with 'hilarious' plastered across the cover these days. If this movie is no more than well-meaning twaddle, then I respect them for saying so. Obviously, I suspect the Chinese video pirates copied and pasted that catchy quote from the internet without bothering to check what it might mean. Either that or they have an excellent sense of humour and presume most locals won't bother reading past the word 'Pitt', which is written in seventy-two point font on the front.

I'm in two minds about *Babel*. I liked *21 Grams* by the same director, Alejandro Gonzalez Iñárritu, but how can I ignore the *Atlanta Journal-Constitution*? I'll pass for now, but I'm not leaving without a bagful of swag. Allow me this forbidden pleasure. I don't get to break international law very often.

Let's see. How about *Flags of Our Fathers*, *Ratatouille*, *The Queen* and *Ocean's 13*? War, comedy, drama and an easy-to-watch thriller – all the bases are covered. I ask 'how much?' by waving the four DVDs around like I'm playing four-card poker with over-sized cards. The vendor says 20 kuai. Sounds like a steal so I pay up and hit the road. Damn! You're supposed to haggle in China. He might have taken 19 kuai. Ah, maybe next time. This seems like the best value purchase of my life.

I'm a little sheepish about walking into the supermarket with illegal DVDs up my t-shirt, but it doesn't seem to bother anybody else. Other punters are brazenly swinging small transparent bags containing pirate movies as they march up the shopping aisle past the legal merchandise. The fresh-faced security guard inside has no interest in cracking down on piracy and seems content to limit his jurisdiction to the rows of checkout tills. His brief is to make sure everybody enters through the channel marked with a big blue arrow, and not via the one with the big red 'X' above it. It's a one-way system which I suspect was devised purely to give the guard something to do.

Supermarkets look pretty similar the world over. The same lighting and colours dominate; the same mix of smells waft up your nose and the music is always familiar but insipid. They are playing a panpipes version of 'Sacrifice' by Elton John over the PA system. 'Imagine' by John Lennon is next, followed by another tune I can't quite put my finger on.

The supermarket's meat counter is not for the fainthearted. Bits of animals that might usually be thrown out or turned into burgers and chicken nuggets are available for purchase. Chicken neck, anyone? How about a bag of tasty duck heads? The minced beef is a much paler colour than I'm used to. It's clear they use fat-tier meat than has become standard in the West. Here, nothing is wasted.

I'm squirted on the back of the ear by a vibrating shellfish. Good shot, if he meant it. These cockles and mussels are alive-o and look desperate to escape. Too late to evolve limbs now, my mollusc friends.

Next to the tray of mussels is a plate of wriggling caterpillars trapped in their own cocoons. They must wish they'd done a shoddier job sealing their own body bags. I'm repulsed but still willing them on in their bid to break away before their number is up. If just one of them would burst out and fly away to freedom flapping colourful new wings it'd be a triumph for the little guy.

There's Elton singing 'Sacrifice' again. That's not even his best work. What about 'Your Song', 'Rocket Man', 'Goodbye Yellow Brick Road'? I'm not a big fan but how did 'Sacrifice' make it big here? Oh, and there's 'Imagine' again. It's a fourteen minute pan-pipe compilation playing on loop. Maybe there are hidden messages in the song selection. Lennon's masterpiece is often touted as a three and a half minute communist manifesto. And the principle of sacrifice can't be a bad thing to instil in the nation. I recognise the third song now. It's 'Fool If You Think It's Over' by Chris Rea. I can't ascribe any hidden state propagandist message to that little classic. There's got to be a subliminal message from the supermarket buried in there urging us to buy things we don't want though. Apropos of nothing, I have a sudden urge to buy the largest available bottle of Coca-Cola.

I stock up on other essentials but can't seem to find antiperspirant. It'll have to wait. I reckon I'll get another couple of days out of my current can but it's still sweltering outside so better not wait too long. The overstaffed checkout means I'm back out the door in no time and heading to the dorm.

I couldn't get the One Child Policy out of my head when trying to drift off to sleep on my purgatorial bed last night. I found myself Googling IVF clinics when I should have been snoring. Honestly, it's not the kind of thing I usually get up to at 4.00 am, but nothing is normal anymore. I find plenty of clinics offering 'family balancing' services – which we can take to mean sex selection – and even come across reports of a hospital bragging about its record numbers of quadruplets. Now that's a special offer: four babies for the price of one.

I scour the internet for an authoritative source on reproductive medicine in China and come across a Dr Ellen Li. She's Chief Obstetrician and Gynaecologist at the Bayley and Jackson Medical Centre in Beijing so I fire off a few questions by email in the hope that she might reply. Dr Li is a serious medic at a serious clinic and has worked in the US so she knows her stuff. I'm optimistic that she might find time for my electronic Q&A, even though I've posed a few sticky questions.

I do the same for a series of private operators, including the ones boasting of multiple births and pre-implantation sex selection. My last target is a high profile Australian fertility clinic which has set up shop in Shanghai. They're a commercial outfit but don't make any wild claims.

Last night's work has paid off. I've now got two emails in my inbox waiting to be electronically torn open. The first is from Dr Ellen Li and she has answered all my queries. First up, I had asked her why IVF is so popular here, but Dr Li points out that a smaller proportion of babies are born through assisted reproduction in China than in Europe. So it may be a growth area but there's still some way to go. Surprisingly, only three Beijing hospitals are officially licensed to offer IVF, but they are all very busy, she says. This is partly because so many people travel from other provinces to see specialists in the capital.

Do all hospitals offer sex selection, I ask? This is only supposed to be done to screen for sex-linked diseases, according to Dr Li, and she elaborates no further. There are laws against it but given the number of clinics I came across which promise to separate the girls from the boys before they're sixteen cells old, the law doesn't appear to be enforced. Then I stray into the murky territory of the

One Child Policy. I had considered leaving this question out in case doctors felt uneasy addressing a political issue. But Dr Li isn't bothered and I sense she has been asked this question a thousand times.

'It is illegal for commercially run clinics to offer this service [multiple births to help get around the One Child policy] ... Also, it is not a hospital's responsibility to enforce the one-child policy, simply to provide a licensed and safe healthcare service.'

So you're not supposed to be advertising promises of quads but at the same time, doctors are not in the business of population control. Finally, I've asked whether obstetric experts have concerns about clinics mouthing off about their capacity to guarantee multiple births, even though this is widely considered unsafe. This, she says, is a 'big concern', not least because it's illegal.

I never hear back from the most commercially-minded clinics. Despite having the glitziest websites and making the most eye-catching claims, they're too busy to field questions. But the second email I've got is from the Australian clinic that has expanded into Shanghai. Their marketing department has set up an interview with the company medical director, Prof Gab Kovacs. I've always felt uneasy about hospitals that have marketing managers but it serves my purpose on this occasion. They've sent Prof Kovacs' profile and he's a serious bloke. I won't bore you with the whole CV but he has been president and chair of all the relevant academic and professional bodies. I have to ring him immediately before he leaves his office and to be honest, I'm a little intimidated. I used to do this kind of thing all the time before I decided to swan off to China but I'm a little out of practise, not to mention under-prepared. I'm expecting an impatient, stuffy old professorial type who'll hang up if I waste a second of his precious time.

It's ringing.

'Oh hello, Professor Kovacs, my name's Gary Finnegan from ...'

'Ah Gary, g'day. How's it going? I heard you were lookin' for me. Call me Gab.'

Gab may be a lofty medical expert but he's still an Aussie – laid back to the last. And he's a helpful bugga. Gab and his mates were approached five years ago by a Shanghai clinic keen to get their success rates up. So the Aussies have been helping them do just that. Demand has been rising but Gab can't say for sure whether it's because the service has improved or more people are turning to IVF.

They don't do pre-implantation genetic diagnosis which can be used to discriminate against female embryos – only a handful of centres have that technology – but they can help with improving the chances of pregnancy, and that can sometimes result in multiple births. That means twins of any gender rather than breeding a five-a-side football team of identical males.

'Our Chinese partner hospital puts back more embryos than they do in our Australian centres – usually two or three.'

'How about quads? Or quins? Some hospitals are doing good business off that kind of promise.'

'Aw no. That'd be crazy. Crazy. It's not safe.'

I'm no expert, but it's worth adding that implanting two or three embryos is no guarantee of twins or triplets. More than one embryo is often implanted in the hope of achieving a single pregnancy. Obviously it can sometimes lead to twins.

My new mate Gab goes on to say that the Shanghai service is for Chinese clients and local expats. They aren't shipping in Australians in search of a cheaper fertility service. In fact, the cost is roughly the same in China as in Australia or Europe. Plus, fertility treatment is not covered by the state so patients pay in cash. Given that salaries are lower here, the relative cost is huge. But the Prof says his experience is that people do whatever it takes to find the money, even if it means working two jobs.

So the twin girls I passed in the park could well be the product of IVF, given that some centres can offer to implant two or three embryos but don't have the technology to choose the sex. Ultrasound will only give you that kind of information when the pregnancy is well underway.

All things considered, it's still more probable that the twins were conceived on a rock-hard Chinese mattress than in a Petri dish.

To take my mind off fertility, I decide to watch a war movie. *Flags of Our Fathers* is one of two films made by Clint Eastwood about the ferocious battle for the Japanese island of Iwo Jima during World War II. Over 20,000 Japanese soldiers died and more than 6,000 US marines and sailors met the same fate. It'll be heavy going but I'm looking forward to it.

The film opens with a warning against piracy. It's theft, you know. A subtitle appears which reads: 'This screener is for your use only. Each copy is digitally fingerprinted ...' and so on. Major film studios fire off scores of these screeners to movie critics to help promote their latest offerings. Oscar season is a particularly good time to pick up high quality bootleg movies because members of the Academy – which selects Oscar nominees – are inundated with movies. Despite their best efforts, studios have yet to balance the need to flood industry insiders with new releases with keeping these copies from falling into the wrong hands.

Unfortunately, the quality of this particular disc is poor. The sound lags three seconds behind the images. It's so far out of sync it's almost unwatchable. I'll leave that one for now and try another.

My copy of the animated comedy *Ratatouille* was clearly recorded from the back of a cinema. When patrons in rows one to five stand up, you can see their heads making a shadow on the screen. Then they bob back across the bottom of the picture holding popcorn and two litres of Pepsi. And you can hear laughter. It's a very authentic home cinema experience. I want to check the quality of the other discs but first I fast forward to the end just to see what happens when the film finishes. Will there be 200 people putting on their coats and shuffling out the door? Nope. The closing credits from an entirely different film have been tacked onto the end instead of the credits from *Ratatouille*. Judging by the credits, the other flick seems to have had more to do with windsurfing than a rat who becomes a master chef.

I've just noticed that the information on the packaging refers to yet another film. It advertises the special features for *Cinderella*. On closer inspection, I find that *Flags of Our Fathers* includes copyright information for the latest *Harry Potter* feature. As long as it looks like an American DVD box, nobody gives a monkey's what it says.

I play the first few promising scenes from *The Queen*, only for the disc to freeze just as I'm getting drawn into the plot. I've wasted a lot of time on these dodgy DVDs and something tells me I'll have my work cut out trying to get a refund from the bootleggers outside the supermarket. Maybe I'll threaten to call the guard.

Come on *Ocean's 13*, don't let me down. It doesn't. The sound and picture are perfect and it looks like it was ripped from a high quality DVD. It's an enjoyable caper and suddenly it doesn't seem like such bad value after all. €2 isn't bad for a top notch DVD. What a great country. For two hours and two minutes, I'm glad I came.

With the US leaning on China to enforce intellectual property law, the golden era of cheap movies may not last forever. That said, I can't imagine things changing much during the twelve months I intend to stay here. And in the unlikely event that there's a sudden clamp down on piracy and the fraud squad attempts a raid on the university, I feel safe knowing there's a 15-year-old guard standing on a box keeping a lookout.

4

Bursting My Bubble

The culture shock has abated but I can't be sure it'll ever disappear completely. I've reduced the nagging voice that screams 'You don't belong here, sonny' to background noise but every so often I feel the volume ratchet up to full blast. It tends to happen when somebody spits near me.

I'm worried. This isn't how it was supposed to be. The plan was that I'd read up on Chinese culture in advance, pick up a few useful phrases and blend in like one of the big global family on arrival. This is supposed to be a personal journey to appreciate eastern culture. And maybe show our distant Chinese cousins that we're all cut from the same cloth; we're all essentially the same, man. 'One love/one life/when it's one need/in the night' as an Irish philosopher once put it.

Well, I'm just not feeling it. Citizen of the world, my arse. Maybe I just can't see past the smog and the spit.

As it happens, you can sign up as to be a World Citizen online for just US$30. They even have their own flag. They'll send you a laminated membership card and tell you you're an integral part of the single giant tapestry that is mankind. But I'm not ready for all that just yet. Lamination is a big commitment. So far I'm seeing more cultural differences than similarities and I'm not feeling terribly connected to my long lost eastern cousins.

Thankfully, I'm not entirely isolated. I have a travelling companion. My dear girlfriend and I are in this together. We both expected to effortlessly assimilate Beijing culture and feel like part of the furniture by the end of our first week. And we're equally disgusted that we've turned out to be a bit softer than we'd fancied ourselves to be.

But we've got to keep plugging away and hope that at some glorious moment we'll break out of our western comfort zone and feel like a pair of locals, albeit big-nosed locals. So it's down a narrow old local laneway for lunch. This is a hive of activity. There are a dozen outdoor hole-in-the-wall eateries, three tiny hair salons and two shops, both alike in pokiness, with public phones sitting atop their narrow counters. There's a lot of spitting and a lot of food preparation, but I'm resisting the temptation to turn my nose up and seek out a restaurant that has its own roof.

It's like I'd been living in a bubble until I stepped off the plane in Beijing. Everything up to that point seemed safe and comfortable. It may have been a false reality; a veneer over the uglier sides of life, but who couldn't enjoy that? Alas, once you cross the Rubicon there's no going back. My innocent eyes have been forever opened. Now that I'm here, I desperately want to embrace the raw, unvarnished real world and immerse myself in a less cosy lifestyle. I've got to unwrap the cotton wool and get a bit of dirt under my fingernails.

'Oh my God, they're roasting cocooned caterpillars on sticks – let's go.'

I decided it was best to ease into this new way of life. It's not so much that I'm a cosseted westerner, it's just that you need to take things slowly or it becomes counterproductive. Too much, too soon, could set us back weeks, you see?

As we head towards a local restaurant with its own tables, chairs and waitresses, Girlfriend declares the whole world to be a bit like Las Vegas. It sounds a bit off the wall and I fear she may have inadvertently gotten high by passively inhaling aerosol solvents hanging in the polluted atmosphere. But I decide to hear her out.

In lavish Vegas hotels, guests exist in a false reality where everything is shiny, safe and easy. But behind the swinging kitchen doors there is a grittier unseen world. That's where the staff, whose manpower fuels the cosy luxury enjoyed by the better off folk in the foyer, stay. Their living quarters are rundown and they work every waking hour for peanuts just to get by. The hotel guests sipping mojitos at the freshly laid felt blackjack table outside are oblivious to life behind those swinging doors. They get intoxicated and retire to their plush suites in the early hours, while the staff accept the hand life's dealt them and set about laying the tables for breakfast.

On a global scale, we, decadent westerners, waltz around the sanitised hotel lobby, sustained by our industrious eastern cousins who toil away out in our peripheral vision hoping one day to get a seat at the roulette table. By coming to China we're chancing a sneaky look through those swinging doors.

I decide to steal her analogy for later use. She won't even remember saying it she's so high on solvents.

We're creating quite a stir in the popular local restaurant we've just walked into. This street isn't exactly a tourist trap so we're a novelty to staff and patrons alike. We are led to a table by a visibly excited waitress and given a twelve-page menu. She walks away for fifteen seconds and returns to take the order. In the meantime, another waitress has positioned herself at one corner of the table and a grinning waiter is standing at the opposite end. I nod nervously at both. Neither seems interested in taking the order, they just want a look. In any case we haven't nearly begun to figure out which of the sixty available meals we want. By the time we have, there are five personnel gathered around us. I point out two dishes in the menu and the team of servers disperses. We used to have a strict rule that restaurants with pictures of their food in the window or on menus are to be avoided. Now it's a prerequisite. Some menus have English translations but others just have Chinese script which I haven't even attempted to learn yet.

The meal arrives and we look at other diners to see how things are done. Everybody gets their own bowl of rice and the main courses are placed in the centre of the table. Using chopsticks or a spoon – I haven't seen a knife and fork since I got here – you help yourself to food, which you're expected to land on your own plate or bowl temporarily, before putting it into your mouth. Unless you're an uncouth savage, you never take food from the serving dish straight to your lip.

It still feels like a long way from the bowl to my mouth when I'm using chopsticks but the percentage of food successfully reaching its destination increases with every meal.

At the table next to us there's a couple silently hunched over their respective rice bowls flicking food into their mouths. Their chins are at table level and they've tipped their bowls towards themselves. It's one hundred per cent efficient, even if it looks a little odd. I'm going to have to completely reformat my existing manners. I'll get some funny looks at home if I forget to switch back when I leave China.

The pork dish we've ordered is mostly lumps of fat sitting in an oily sauce on a garden of new potatoes. I'm wishing I could dissect the meat with a sharp knife. Chopsticks just aren't practical for that kind of thing. Of course, everybody else is untroubled by this basic chopstick design flaw. They are eating everything in front of them without discrimination or dissection.

The second thing I had pointed to was meant to be a vegetable dish but actually comes with bits of ground minced beef sprinkled through the broccoli. I like it, but a vegetarian wouldn't. Vegetarianism is not a concept Chinese people have really bought into. Given that food hasn't always been so plentiful – and still isn't in some provinces – they must find the idea of bringing your moral code to the dinner table quite alien. Fussiness is a luxury.

I didn't eat much pig fat but the broccoli *con carne* hit the spot. The spuds that accompanied the pork are polished off purely because we're hungry. They don't taste like the potatoes we were reared on, but with a bit of oily sauce they're not the worst. Eating in Beijing can be hit and miss. I was looking forward to getting stuck into Chinese food but when you haven't a clue what you're ordering it's a risky business. Once we've compiled a mental list of palatable dishes things should improve. The broccoli is added to that list.

I use the universal gesture for 'Can I have the bill please' – pretending to scribble on an imaginary sheet of paper – and say 'mai dan' in a most unconvincing tone. 'Mai dan' means 'bill'. It's one of my two dozen words.

Dinner for two, with a few bottles of local beer, costs 37 kuai, roughly €3.70. It might have cost one quarter of that down the alley from which we earlier fled, but we're working up to that, remember?

We're still well under our daily budget so I'm splashing out on a haircut. Restaurants close pretty early in this neighbourhood but you can get your locks shorn at almost any hour of the day or night. And there's no shortage of hairdressers.

You can tell a lot about a city by the types of shops that dominate its streets. Here, it's all banks and hair salons. There's a bank on every second corner but the queues are legendary. You take a number and a seat until you're called. There might be 150 tickets between you and the teller. I opened an account this morning and was apparently fortunate to be in and out in less than ninety minutes. Lucky me.

Maybe Chinese people are reluctant to trust online banking but it seems like banks are the busiest places in town. There must be a lot of cash floating around – a sign of how China has been changing. The plethora of hairdressers is an index of new China's lust for self-improvement. Now that the whole world is looking at Beijing, she wants to look her best.

I choose the quietest looking salon on the street. The others are blaring Asian rock music and are full of trendies with two-tone hair. That's not my scene.

I walk in to find the hairdresser asleep on a couch with the headphones of an MP3 player in her ears. The young sweeper-upper is glued to the TV in the top corner of the room which is showing soap operas. There's an old man with no obvious purpose languidly pacing the white-tiled floor, sighing and spitting. Maybe I could have put up with the Asian rock.

There's an open scissors covered in hair on a glass shelf, sitting next to a pair of combs which appear to be stuck to each other. I don't see any of the sterilising units that hang from the walls of the barber shops I'm accustomed to. Fair enough; things are different here, I remind myself. I say 'ni hao' and the hairdresser drags herself off the couch and utters a string of sounds that I presume equates roughly to 'D'ye want much off the top?'

I manage to communicate that I want about 'this much' removed from my locks. And so it begins.

The sweeper-upper unnerves me by standing at my shoulder with a fixed smile on her face throughout. She never says a word. I smile back awkwardly but it has no effect on her expression. I try frowning. Not a flicker.

The hairdresser speaks again and points at my glasses. I remove them eagerly and semi-apologetically. I have shockingly bad eyesight. It now dawns on me that I can neither speak to those around me, nor can I see what's going on. I place my blind faith in the hands of an overtired girl with a scissors in her hand.

She sets about rapidly combing and cutting; shaving and yawning. The comb is sticky with old gel and it pulls my hair. It hurts a little but I say nothing. I'm very brave.

The razor roars past where my sideburns used to be and then around my neck. The sleepy hairdresser shaves down the nape of my neck to a certain point but then notices more stray hairs just below my collar. Pulling back the shirt, she shaves some more, but realises there are even more hairs to be found – and they are all attached. A look is exchanged between the cutter and the sweeper but I can't make out what it is. I'm presuming they think I'm the missing link. Chinese men are not very hairy and even by European standards I'm probably a little hirsute. It's more the unusual distribution than the number of hairs that makes me special.

Anyway, it's time to pay. That's one of the fastest but most thorough haircuts I've ever had. The hairdresser flashes all five fingers several times. Does she want 15 or 50? I ask in dodgy Mandarin if she means 50 kuai. She doesn't. She means five. The old codger in the corner pipes up: '50 kuai, 50 kuai' and falls around laughing. Naive Big Nose that I am, I would have paid it.

So the haircut sets me back about 50 cent. Now that's value. The day I got too old for the £3 student special in Stephen's Barbershop around the corner from where I grew up, I reckoned I'd never again get such a great cut for less than the price of a pint. You'd barely get a pint of milk for 50 cent. But I won't complain. The market is saturated and Sleepy has contained her costs by cutting down on hygiene products.

The living is easy outside the central commercial and tourist districts of the city but tomorrow I'm paying a visit to Beijing's busiest shopping street so we'll see how far my yuan stretches there.

I hop on the subway at Yuquanlu – my local station – parting with two kuai for a ticket as I do so. I'm up bright and early by my standards, although Beijingers already have half a day's work done. It's early to bed and early to rise in China's capital. And, true enough, they seem healthy, they're getting wealthy and I'm sure some are wise.

The train is stuffy, crowded and smelly. And it makes me feel right at home. Public transport is like this everywhere. There's a fan blowing above my head but it's having minimal impact on the humidity. Subway Line 1 runs a straight track from where I live to Wangfujing, via Tiananmen Square, and beyond. Wangfujing Street is where I'm headed and I'm looking forward to being in the thick of things.

The subway network is surprisingly sparse for a city of fifteen million people. Line 1 bisects the city horizontally and Line 2 runs in a loop around the centre. Grafted on top of that is Line 13 which makes an arc around the city's northern districts and links into Line 2. The newest addition is Line 5 which runs from north to south and intersects with all three of the other tracks. Line 5 stations look a little more swish than the others, but I'm sure they'll all get that lived-in look in no time. More lines are planned but as things stand, the system is a lot less comprehensive than the Paris Metro, London Tube or any other comparably large city you care to think of.

The distance between stops is considerable so it takes half an hour to get to Wangfujing.

From the foot of the subway station stairs, the city smog is already filling my lungs. Skyscrapers disappear up into the clouds while gridlocked traffic belches out more fumes. This is Beijing alright. I take my life in my hands crossing the broad boulevard and manage to make it to the relative safety of Wangfujing Street. It's pedestrianised but I'll keep my wits about me all the same in case a lunatic on a three-wheeler decides to take a shortcut through the crowds.

I never visited Soviet Russia and by the time I got to the beautiful old cities of Eastern Europe, communism had collapsed. Nonetheless, I'm going to stick my neck out and speculate that communism never looked so neon as it does here. If you just focus on the billboards and brand names, you could be in any modern city in the western world. The Chinese government describes what's happening here as 'socialism with Chinese characteristics'. They trot out this phrase *ad nauseum* just in case anybody gets the mad notion that China has embraced capitalism. They may not have democracy in Beijing, but there's a swelling middle class and they are buying up global brands and drinking Starbucks frappuccinos. Consumerism is king of this communist state.

Wangfujing Street was completely revamped in 1999 at a cost of one billion yuan or €100 million. I can't imagine what all these manic shopaholics did until then. It now boasts several large shopping malls where all the biggest international chains have a presence. There's a Starbucks, of course, and an incredibly expensive movie theatre. Faced with Draconian censorship and unbeatable competition, cinema has taken a bit of a battering in China. In a land where pirated DVDs are available for five kuai, who would pay 70 kuai for the pleasure of sitting in front of the silver screen? Not me, obviously.

The cost of clothes in the top shops is surprisingly similar to Europe. And to afford European prices you need to be earning European wages. There are plenty of people on good money in Beijing today but the average wage is around 4,000 kuai a month. You wouldn't want to make a habit of splashing out 1,200 for a pair of designer jeans.

I grab lunch in a blindingly well-lit restaurant on 'Gourmet Street' inside one of the malls. My chicken curry is an unmitigated disappointment. There appear to be two fried chicken feet standing on top of the dish when it arrives. I tell myself these are plastic decorations (they aren't) and set them to one side with my chopsticks. I don't find much in the way of white meat, and chopsticks are still useless when faced with so much skin and bone. I try to gnaw some flesh from a slippery chicken wing but abandon the project after frustration gets the better of me. I grumpily pour the curry sauce into my rice bowl – not caring whether it's a dining *faux pas* – and make the best of it. There's nothing like a gastronomic letdown to put you in a bad mood.

The bill comes to 72 kuai, roughly double what we'd paid for two meals the night before. Lesson learnt.

Now if I had been braver, I'd have headed straight for the famed Wangfujing snack street. I pay it a visit but I'm not in the market for what's on sale there.

Taking a left under an ornate archway off the main Wangfujing Street, the open air snack street serves up pork and cabbage dumplings; rice balls filled with sweetened bean paste; stewed pig's intestine; and, of course, a whole host of insects on sticks. You can get six roasted baby scorpions skewered if you like. But I don't.

I walk in a horseshoe shape around the narrow lanes and re-emerge further up the main street right next to one of the shops I've been most keen to visit.

The Foreign Language Bookstore is one of a handful of places in Beijing where a good range of English-language reading material can be found. On the upper floors you can find English DVDs, including TV series. They are mad for *Prison Break* and *Lost* here, but I can't find *Sopranos* or *The Wire*. And there's a legal copy of *Babel* at the relatively cheap price of 30 kuai. I buy it. At least I can be sure it'll work.

I had been playing Spot the Big Nose on my way up the street but it's like shooting fish in a barrel in here. The bookshops are packed with foreigners but otherwise I've been surprised at the relatively low numbers of tourists in the shopping malls. Maybe everybody is queuing up to get into the Forbidden City – where I plan to go next week – or maybe it's because the clothes on sale on Beijing's high street are identical to what's on offer at home.

I leave the Foreign Language Bookstore and make my way to the large Chinese bookshop on Wangfujing. It reveals an overwhelming appetite for books about business. Literature is very much taking a back seat. There are separate sections on finance, management, economics, sales, and enterprise development. This must be another indicator of China's obsession with self-improvement and its embrace of the market economy.

So that's banks, hairdressers and shops packed with business books. I might conclude that the future of China is a generation of high-rolling consumers addicted to personal development and having great hair. But I don't like to rush to judgement.

Between the smog, the heat and the overcrowding, I'm thinking of calling it a day. I seek refuge in a gorgeously air-conditioned electronics store, selling all the latest in sleek gadgetry. They've got iPods and palmtops, laptops and camera phones. I could do with a charger for my phone, so I have a casual browse, taking care to drag out this air-conditioned bliss for as long as possible.

It turns out I'm excellent at haggling in China. This comes as quite a surprise because I'd usually be more likely to apologise for bidding offensively low than to drive a hard bargain. Maybe this is the new hardnosed me.

The trick seems to be to con yourself into not really wanting whatever is on offer. The charger I was looking at was marked 280 kuai. I presume this to be the actual price and dismiss any thought of buying it. You don't haggle in a plush high street shop that sells iBooks, do you? I must have dwelled too long thinking about it because I've drawn the attention of two sales assistants. More overstaffing.

'You'll buy it?' they ask. I tell them, politely, that I'll think about it, and try to shuffle off.

'How much you pay?'

I really don't want to get into a haggling situation – which is the key to successful negotiation, remember – so I just say I'd prefer to have a look around the other shops and might pop back in an hour or so.

'How much, how much? What is your price?'

I'm trying to walk away but they are insistent. Eventually I say I had hoped to part with around 100 kuai. That should get them off my case. But it doesn't. They suggest 150 kuai. I'm really not that pushed about the charger so I turn to leave.

And they cave. 'Okay 100 kuai,' they sigh, typing the number into their calculator to show me. Fair enough. I buy it before they change their minds.

Now, did I save myself 180 kuai or have they just sold something to a Big Nose that he didn't really want?

I'm still peckish having not eaten much of my overpriced chicken skin 'n' bone curry, but can't bring myself to venture back down snack street as I make for the subway station. Before I arrived in Beijing, the international media was full of stories about China's deplorable safety standards. If it wasn't lead paint on Barbie dolls, it was carcinogenic food colouring. Pesticides were found in toothpaste, antifreeze detected in prescription medicines and a lethal coal derivative somehow found its way into millions of cans of pet food. No negative press on scorpion sticks though.

China is worried, not least about the reputation of its exported goods, while the US has had a field day highlighting the apparently low quality of Chinese produce. So what did Beijing bigwigs do to prove they were taking the problem seriously? They shot a man in the head. Yep, they couldn't have their global trading partners thinking China is a wild, backward state. So they expeditiously charged and convicted the head of the State Food and Drug Administration with taking bribes from pharmaceutical companies and issued a press release claiming they were on top of the situation.

A corrupt Communist Party official? It's shocking. Off with his head!

With great efficiency, Zheng Xiaoyu was sentenced to death, shot, and a new official installed in his old office. I hope the new guy knows what he's doing. It must be quite an incentive to think that your predecessor misused his power and now he's worm food.

I'm not sure whether the new trigger-happy approach to food safety standards should instil confidence or fear. The general standards prevailing in China have been on my mind since I arrived. In the West, there is a general expectation that competent authorities will keep us safe from harm. And, with the exception of the occasional lapse, that's how it is. Food, medicines, toys, electronics, water quality – they're regulated. Companies live in a healthy fear of losing their reputation or winding up in front of a judge. That sort of accountability is emerging in China but it's not here yet. As a result, I find myself holding back on living like a local. What if the caterpillars are only half-cooked? What if medicines are just sugar and baking soda? Who do I call when the water tastes metallic?

I don't think I'm this paranoid and fussy at home. What's more, I was hoping that I'd feel increasingly eastern with every passing day. If anything, I'm feeling more western than ever. Having started out as an easygoing Irishman, I seem to have psychologically drifted further west and become more precious than I'd ever thought possible.

Oh sweet mother of Jesus – I'm turning into an American.

5

Mao Country

J walk by two old but athletic-looking men wearing vests which they've pulled up to just below their nipples. It would be indecent to hoist a vest any higher, I suppose.

This is a common sight in Beijing during the summer months. Men regularly walk around with their shirts hitched above their bellies to keep themselves cool. The sight of a sixty-year-old with his t-shirt tied up in a bow demands a double-take first time around, but you get used to it. That said, it's unlikely to be a style I'll adopt, no matter how much I embrace Chinese culture.

A gigantic dragonfly whizzes past my head as I look up at the eight-storey cuboid building that I will call home for the next eleven months. I duck to avoid the flying monster as it performs erratic loop-de-loops around the branch of a cypress tree. Girlfriend and I are about to get our first look at our new apartment. It's on the university campus where we'll both be working, which is uncharacteristically leafy for Beijing. Of course where there's greenery, you'll find dragonflies as big as bats but it's a price worth paying. Dragonflies are harmless freaks – although, I will continue to duck every time I find myself in their flight path – and the green leaves make the smoggy air a little more breathable.

We're taken to a newly renovated top floor flat by the ever-helpful Mr Xie from the college's International Affairs Office. He's a Mr Fix-it for the foreign staff, who sorts out visas, banking and accommodation.

The door swings open to reveal a narrow living room with green tiles and bare white walls. There are no wooden skirting boards but they've painted a blue band around the base of the walls so it initially looks as though there are. There's dust every-where from the refurbishment work which looks like it finished about twenty minutes ago. There's a microwave and one portable electronic hob but no oven. The tap spews out rancid brown water which spills onto the floor beneath the sink. I try to contain my displeasure at the state of the apartment, partly because there's no second option and partly because I don't like making a fuss. If Mr Xie had shown me to a barn door and said it was the best they could manage, I'd probably have smiled politely and said it was 'grand'. Our new home isn't exactly what we'd hoped for but I tell Mr Xie we'll be fine from here and he leaves us to it.

This used to be a corridor full of student dorms but they have just finished merging two dorm rooms into single apartments for teachers. Apparently six students used to live in the space that I consider rather compact. I can't imagine how it must have smelled.

This place is a marvel of design. They clearly put approxi-mately zero thought into how the available space could best be used. It doesn't appear to have benefited from the wonders of Computer Aided Design, or even a t-square and pencil for that matter. They just marched in with a list of things an apartment should have and set about randomly installing same. The TV is in the living room but the only connection point for the cable is in the kitchen. This means I'll need an eight metre cable running be-tween rooms and won't be able to close the sliding glass door that should separate the living room from the kitchen.

The bathroom displays an equal investment of thought. The toilet and shower are in separate cubicles, which isn't a problem. But the shower room features a large hot water tank at head height, making it a little tricky to stand up straight. The tank has to be plugged into one of two sockets in the bathroom, both of which look equally likely to get wet. I've never ever seen a socket in a bathroom so this feeds into the 'they-have-no-safety-standards-in-China' narrative that continues to swirl around the front of my consciousness.

Everything is finished to the lowest of standards. The kitchen sink is joined to the worktop by thick blobs of dried glue and there's an ill-fitting hose running from underneath the sink to the drain. It looks like they were missing a pipe so they grabbed the tube from an old vacuum cleaner and rammed it into the sink. The connection where the hose meets the sink is not sealed, which explains why there is now a pool of brown water sloshing around our floor. There are open shores in the kitchen, bathroom and shower cubicle, which might account for the healthy population of cockroaches.

The bed is the best part – or am I just tired? It's huge and comparatively soft. By the standards I was used to until a couple of weeks ago it would probably be considered too firm, but it'll be like sleeping on air after my fortnight on the steel prison bed.

It seems my standards are slipping. That's a great sign. Now if I could just lower my expectations for clean air and safe food I'd be half-way to total immersion.

By Beijing standards an eight-floor building is low-rise. The ground below boasts plenty of trees, but the skyline is a sea of cranes, half-built apartment blocks, and scaffolding covered in green gauze. This is a city under construction and renovation. I expect the view to have transformed completely by the time I'm packing my bags to leave next year.

The living quarters are a little cramped and the rising skyline makes for a claustrophobic vista so where better to escape to than the world's largest open urban space: Tiananmen Square.

So vast is Tiananmen that it has two subway stops both of which leave you in the thick of things. I opt for Tiananmen East and pop up from the subterranean station to a hectic scene of tourists and guards, flashing cameras and surveying the scene, respectively. The expansive, history-heavy square is a hive of activity this afternoon as I pan across its 109 concrete acres. It is 880 metres from south to north and 500 metres east to west. The square was originally built in 1417 by the Ming Dynasty and renovated in 1699 by the Qing Dynasty. However it was crammed with civic offices and went through several metamorphoses before being expanded by Chairman Mao Zedong and his communist comrades after they took power in 1949.

These days Mao's portrait hangs above the north gate of the square and his body rests in a mausoleum where the Chinese can pay their respects and foreign tourists can file past wondering how this guy managed to pull off such a stunning publicity coup.

Mao is central to the Chinese psyche. He's on every note of legal tender and embellished stories of his greatness abound. It is he who the Chinese thank and praise for ending centuries of division within and threat from without.

Alas, Mao also made some catastrophic errors of judgement during his time in power but given the frenzy of young Chinese eager to be photographed under the benevolent gaze of his portrait this seems to have gone unnoticed. Against all odds, he created and nurtured a personality cult that would rival anything Hitler, Stalin or Castro could dream up. (Apologies to Fidel for lumping him in with such detestable company.)

Mao is portrayed as a revolutionary genius in China. He's a visionary, a military strategist, a reformer, a poet and a master calligrapher. Is there anything he couldn't do? Unfortunately, he had plenty of failings but these have been largely airbrushed out of Chinese history.

In the face of external criticism of Mao's reign, the official line in recent years has been to tweak the traditional portrayal of Mao as an infallible maverick. The new truth, according to the Party, is that Chairman Mao made a great contribution to the development of the People's Republic – and he was seventy per cent right and thirty per cent wrong. Officially. That's still a lot of wrong. If he tossed a coin for every decision, he'd still have made it to fifty per cent right. He wouldn't be your first choice in *Fantasy Who Wants to be a Millionaire?* (I'd take one of the popes if I had to choose.)

Assembling any kind of balanced picture of Mao is tricky, especially from within China. He is a demigod here, but his bad reputation overseas was also coloured by anti-communist propaganda from the US during the cold war. I'm entering a subjective world of multiple truths here, but my own estimates suggest I'm usually eighty-four per cent accurate, so this should be close enough to the centre ground. I can promise you that he was born in 1893 and died in 1976. In that time he almost certainly married four women, if you count an arranged marriage, and fought with the revolutionaries that overthrew the Qing Dynasty in 1911. That marked the end of dynastic rule in China and the birth of the Republic of China. He educated himself reasonably well, partly by sitting in on lectures at Beijing University, even though he wasn't registered.

The Republic of China was to last from 1911 to 1949 when Mao and the communists won a bloody civil war and founded the People's Republic of China. Mao was attracted by the ideas of Marx and Lenin in his twenties and got in on the ground floor by attending the first meeting of the Communist Party of China in Shanghai in 1921. He rapidly rose through the ranks but was forced to lead his local branch of the Kuomintang, the nationalist political party which governed China and would eventually become Mao's foe in the civil war. He served as Acting Propaganda Director of the Kuomintang in 1925 and 1926, where he clearly picked up a trick or two.

Mao admired Soviet communism but as the son of a farmer, he preferred to dream of an uprising led by rural peasants rather than an urban proletariat movement. He also came to believe a violent revolution was the best way to achieve his ends. Peaceful revolution is underrated.

It sounds a little bizarre but Mao established what he called the Soviet Republic of China in 1931 in the mountainous region of Jiangxi. The rest of China was still under the control of the Kuomintang and would remain so for the best part of two decades. To my mind, that's a bit like camping out in the Wicklow Mountains with a big gang of friends and deciding to declare it a country. But it was a symbolic move and gave the future Chairman a taste of power. He learned how to suppress local opponents and developed a reputation for unflinching torture. There's no need for gruesome detail here. It's enough to say that if you can arrange the words 'red-hot', 'gun-rod', 'rammed' and 'anus' in the most painful conceivable order you'll have enough to go on.

It was during this spell that Mao formed his Red Army. It relied on guerrilla warfare to a large degree in its early battles with the Kuomintang, but after World War II Mao's men were armed by the Soviets while the US supported the Kuomintang. The Red Army won major victories in early 1949 and by December of that year the Kuomintang leaders had fled to Taiwan. China became a communist state.

Little Mao 'son-of-a-peasant' Zedong had grown up to become the most powerful man in China having led the nationwide socialist revolution. And what was the first instinct of this people's champion when he installed himself in a compound next to the palatial Forbidden City? 'Build me a swimming pool'!

He was dead right. What sort of palace doesn't have an indoor pool? He ordered the construction of several other luxurious new buildings and also earned a reputation for conducting his business affairs either in bed or by the poolside. He preferred not to wear formal dress unless he absolutely had to. Everyday was Casual Friday for the Chairman.

When you come to power after a civil war, it seems customary to purge your enemies. And that's just what Mao set about doing. In tandem with his land reforms, he ordered mass executions of his opponents, killing between 700,000 and 1,000,000 people. He had a policy that at least one landlord in every village should be publicly executed. Later estimates put the total death toll for Mao's first few years at around 5,000,000. That's like slaughtering the entire population of Ireland in half a decade. Some lucky sods were spared and sent to camps where they could hope to achieve 'reform through labour'. Many died there, others emerged as committed communists.

Mao rolled out his first five year plan in 1953. How very organised of him. What's my five year plan? What's my one year plan? What am I doing next Thursday? I'll never be a supreme leader if I don't get my act together.

His first attempt to end China's dependence on land saw huge numbers of industrial plants being built with a little help from Russia. It was a relatively successful five years – at least when compared with what was to follow.

Brimming with overconfidence, Chairman Mao unfurled another five year plan in 1958 which he dubbed 'The Great Leap Forward'. He'd obviously never heard of temping fate.

Small farms were merged into large agricultural communes and peasants were ordered to work on large-scale infrastructure projects. Targets for the production of steel were set and everybody was to do their part, melting down whatever they could in makeshift furnaces. Private food production was banned, while farm machinery and livestock were brought under collective ownership. Mao and his cronies also imposed their own unproven and unscientific agricultural techniques for farmers.

So that's political revolution, poetry, calligraphy, swimming and agri-science – Mao was a Jack of all trades. Unfortunately, his plan was far from masterful.

The results were devastating. Grain production fell by fifteen per cent in 1959 and by a further ten per cent in 1960. It's likely that the Chairman didn't know the extent of his own failure. Party officials, fearing the wrath of their superiors, inflated figures for crop yields to please their bosses. 'Oh, things are goin' great here, boss – no problems at all.'

By the time word trickled up to Mao at the top of the pyramid, things would have looked pretty rosy. Food was brought from the countryside to the cities and China continued to be a net exporter of grain. All the while, rural peasants – Mao's revolutionary heroes – starved in their millions. The Great Leap ended in 1962 and Mao lost face with party colleagues. Only his own propaganda-fuelled popularity kept him in power.

As if the starving masses weren't bad enough, the wheels began to fall off the infrastructural projects and the steel production plan. The steel quotas were reached all right, so that's success of a sort, but the metal was produced by untrained rural workers who had been ordered to switch from farming to industrial steel work. Much of what was produced were useless hunks of junk which had been melted down in homemade furnaces from scrap metal. The infrastructural work was equally fruitless, primarily because Mao had rejected input from trained engineers because those know-it-all professionals were elitist bastards.

So he had taken skilled farmers off the land and ordered them to turn their hands to bridge building. In hindsight, it's not too surprising that agriculture and infrastructure flat-lined.

At the CCP conference in 1962 several brave colleagues pointed out that the Great Leap hadn't taken China as far forward as had been promised. Liu Shaoqui and Deng Xiaoping, who were State President and General Secretary respectively, took matters in hand and attempted a damage limitation exercise. The agri-communes were disbanded, small peasant farm holdings and some private control was re-introduced and grain was imported from Canada and Australia. Despite the fact that China's hierarchy included several progressive thinkers like Deng Xiaoping, who would eventually take control in 1978, Mao managed to hold firm and reasserted his power in the mid-1960s.

To rescue is own legacy and quash dissent, Mao felt the need for another grand project. In 1966 the Cultural Revolution was launched. This was effectively a brutal clampdown on so-called bourgeois liberals who were seen as a threat to the socialist paradise Mao was building. Sweeping powers were handed to the Red Army – a motley crew of uniformed teenagers – who set up their own tribunals, closed schools and ordered intellectuals to leave cities. Huge numbers of citizens were imprisoned, China's cultural heritage was decimated and economic and social chaos ensued. Violence and suicide soared. The hellish Cultural Revolution ended in 1969 but not before the nation had been turned on its head.

Miraculously, Mao's popularity was enduring. Regardless of what went wrong, there was always somebody else to blame – the weather, local officials, the Japanese – but never the man at the top.

The Party faithful and other good citizens carried around his Little Red Book of quotations like a Bible. The book is packed with selected samples of the Chairman's wisdom on just about every topic imaginable. And it includes some handy practical advice: 'In waking of tiger use a long stick.' Noted.

But some of his pronouncements on accepting constructive criticism seem a little empty considering how he put down opponents. 'If we have shortcomings, we are not afraid to have them pointed out and criticised, because we serve the people. Anyone, no matter who, may point out our shortcomings. If he is right, we will correct them.' Maybe he went on to say '... and then we'll send them to labour camps', but this was removed by savvy editors. The predominant themes throughout the Little Red Book are violent revolution, people power and *sacrifice* for the greater good. That's surely why Elton John's 1990 hit is so popular.

Standing in Tiananmen Square, the most pertinent quotation might be Mao's declaration that China's youth will control the future. 'The world belongs to you. China's future belongs to you.'

I'm struck by the number of guards in Tiananmen. And that's just the visible police presence. Scores of plain clothes officers are also dispersed through the crowds watching for the first hint of trouble. These guys are not here to protect tourists from pickpockets. They are here to sniff out the first whiff of political dissent. I wish they'd do something about the number of bogus tour guides pestering big-nosed foreigners. You can't move in Tiananmen Square without being approached by a smiling young Chinese student holding a parasol.

There are two main strategies adopted by these so-called students. Both begin with an upbeat greeting – 'Hello, where are you from? America? England?' – to which you should never respond. The first tactic is to introduce themselves as a tour guide. They say they are English students and, for a small fee, will give you a private tour of the Square, the Forbidden City, or even the Great Wall which is over fifty miles away. The tour transpires to be expensive and you may also be led to overpriced restaurants where you'll be fleeced for every penny you've got.

Scam two is for gullible art lovers. The con artist claims to be a student of design or fine art and invites you to an 'exclusive exhibition'. When you get there you'll be badgered into buying paintings you neither need nor want. Your only strategy as a tourist when these schemers home in on you has to be a stony-faced forward glare. Under no circumstances should you make eye contact or say 'no thank you'. Certainly don't engage in civil conversation or you'll never escape.

It's not impossible that one or two of these students really are tour guides or students who just want to practise their English, but I've yet to hear a story beginning with 'A friendly girl with a parasol approached us in Tiananmen' that doesn't end with 'What a rip off!'

I cross the bridge at Tiananmen's north gate and walk under the arch where Mao's portrait hangs. I've been amusing myself with what I suspect is the easiest game going: Spot the Undercover Policeman. Of course, there's no way of confirming your suspicions when you think you've spotted a spy. But when you see a dour, middle-aged man with no camera, no family and no apparent purpose, it's a dead giveaway. If he's standing with his hands behind his back and his eyes on everyone else's business, that's the clincher. They are ten-a-penny so I give up and silently survey the scene with my hands clenched behind me. If it wasn't for the big nose, you'd think I was undercover.

There's a man collecting plastic bottles from tourists under the arch, and he has been having a great day. He must have hundreds of bottles in his old woven sack and has been selling miniature Chinese flags as a sideline. I can hear him spitting like a madman as I turn to face the Square and take in the sprawling scale of the open space. The spitting isn't bothering me much today. It's the throat clearing that's getting on my wick. The sound of phlegm being hacked up into the mouth for projectile release − like the trigger of a loaded gun being cocked − gives me shivers. The actual emission of gooey spittle comes as something of a relief. It's when you hear hacking which isn't followed by the anticipated spit that the stomach really turns.

Blocking out the hustling tour guides and bustling tourists, Tiananmen is quite a sight. It has been the scene of joyous celebrations as well as untold horrors. The Square is remembered by the Chinese people for the proclamation of the People's Republic of China in 1949, but the rest of the world has another image embossed on its collective memory.

In 1989, social unrest which had been quietly stirring for a number of years came to a head in Beijing. China was changing.

By the 1980s it had effectively abandoned Maoist ideology and was opening up to the global economy. But not everybody was happy with the results. Intellectuals and students felt social reform was too slow. Industrial workers on the other hand were unhappy with some of the economic changes which had fuelled inflation and unemployment.

In April of that year, small gatherings of students and academics snowballed, leading to hundreds of thousands marching on Tiananmen Square. Rallies began springing up in Xi'an and Changsha, and concerns within the Party grew. Communism was on its last legs in the Soviet Union and across Eastern Europe, and the Chinese government feared it could be washed away in a worldwide democratic wave if things got out of hand.

The protests gathered momentum with rallies against corruption and demands for freedom of the press. Over the course of a few weeks, the demonstrations were becoming bigger and louder, with some demanding the end of Communist Party rule altogether.

Despite its initial resistance to use force, the government eventually crushed the protests in the early hours of the fourth of June. The death toll has been estimated at anything from 300 to 3,000, depending on whether you trust the figures tallied by the government or by Chinese students' associations. *The New York Times* settled on 400 to 800 deaths.

The most enduring image of this traumatic period is of a lone man in a white shirt blocking the progress of a column of tanks as the army rolled out of Tiananmen Square. The leading tank tried to drive around him but the skinny young rebel moved into its path. He then stood defiantly for a moment before climbing on top of the tank's turret to shout at the soldiers. The tanks stood still until an onlooker pulled the young man back into the crowd. His identity remains unknown, as does his fate. Some say he is still alive and well, while others believe he was executed two weeks later during a ruthless purge.

Remarkably, the whole episode has been wiped out of Chinese history. It's not recorded in textbooks or referenced in newspapers. The date '6/4' doesn't resonate the way other historically significant dates do for Chinese people – or the way '9/11' is remembered in the US and beyond. If you are bold enough to raise the subject of the Tiananmen Square protests – or the 'massacre' as some western media prefer – you will get blank looks. It's not just that it's taboo; people genuinely won't know what you're talking about. If you go online or look through newspaper archives, it's as if '6/4' never happened.

Back in the here and now, I'm wandering towards the cobbles of the Forbidden City wondering if students would ever attempt a repeat of the Tiananmen protests. There doesn't appear to be much appetite for political dissent these days, especially while China is on the up.

Maybe I can stoke up a bit of the old protest spirit back on the university campus. I'll start with a self-serving campaign for better staff accommodation and urgent calls for the introduction of on-the-spot spitting fines. Then again, I'm not sure violent revolution is really my thing. And being purged would suit me much less. It's probably best if I don't make a fuss.

A few hundred yards north of Tiananmen, the Forbidden City compound awaits but first there's another tiny museum in the courtyard drawing my attention.

6

Dynasties

What had you done by the time you were three years old? I was just about getting the hang of potty training and struggling to memorise a few nursery rhymes. Nothing worth putting on the CV.

But for a Beijing toddler named Puyi, life was a little more complicated. In fact he passed the peak of his powers before he was out of short trousers. In 1908, at the tender age of two years and ten months, Puyi became emperor of China. He ascended to the throne after his uncle died, and was to become China's last emperor. However, it wasn't as if he led an army of rugrats to the Forbidden City to seize power – his role was purely symbolic.

Puyi was as distraught as any preschooler to be snatched from his mother's arms and taken to the palace when the imperial vacancy arose. From his point of view it was more of a kidnapping than a power grab. He wasn't to see his mother again for six years, by which time his empire would be unrecognisable.

I'm standing in the tiny one-room museum dedicated to Puyi in the courtyard just south of the tourist-thronged entrance to the Forbidden City. It's a claustrophobic, haphazard display but fascinating in spite of it all. The only staff is a seated woman resting her head on a desk. The walls are covered in badly organised photographs of Puyi taken during his childhood, and more photos from the later years of his bizarre and winding life story. The museum takes on a distinctly red-tinged view of the past. Puyi eventually embraced communism so his reputation is spared but some of those around him are freely derided. Communists generally don't have much time for monarchs.

Puyi, the last emperor, was overthrown in the 1911 revolution which gave birth to the Republic of China. However, he was allowed retain his title even though he had no real power. He was still only six at that stage. Along with his staff and teachers, Puyi remained in the northern half of the Forbidden City and the Summer Palace where he lived a privileged but abnormal life. The Emperor was well educated and had a strong interest in western culture. He married two women when he was 16 and had married three more by the end of his life. Despite having so many wives and concubines, he had no children. One of his sisters-in-law, of which he presumably had very many, reported that he also kept a male concubine and was rather fond of his page boy. It seems probable that Puyi was bisexual or gay, and that's without passing comment on his penchant for dressing up in top hats and patent leather boots for no particular reason.

But his idyllic lifestyle was interrupted by aggressive warlords who were jockeying for position during a turbulent time in Chinese history. In 1917, one such military commander managed to restore Puyi to the throne for all of twelve days. I don't suppose it made much difference to his daily life given that he didn't even hold on to power for a fortnight. Yet another warlord had a more profound impact on the precocious Puyi when he expelled him from the Forbidden City in 1924. The eighteen-year-old former sovereign found refuge in the Japanese concession in Tianjin and was later installed as leader of the government of Manchukuo, which was effectively ruled from Japan. His job was simply to sign off on laws passed by his colonial masters, which saw his regime branded as a puppet government. After such a promising start to what was meant to be a life of power and privilege, Puyi's standing in China was low.

Worse was to follow. After the Second World War ended in 1945, Puyi was captured by the Soviet Red Army and imprisoned in Russia. Meanwhile, back in China, the civil war was under way which would see Mao's communists come to power. Puyi wrote to Joseph Stalin in 1949 begging not to be sent back to the newly established People's Republic of China. But Stalin, not renowned for his compassion, didn't listen. Puyi, the last ruler of dynastic China, was handed over to Beijing's fledgling communist leadership. At a time when Mao's henchmen were mercilessly weeding out all remnants of past powers, it was perhaps a little surprising that Puyi was spared. Just to show they hadn't gone soft, the communists sent him to a 're-education camp' for ten years.

The museum gets carried away with Maoist hysteria at this point, claiming Puyi saw the light while he was in prison and his hitherto haywire brain had been corrected thanks to books by Marx and Lenin, and of course Mao. Mao declared Puyi to have been 'reformed', and in 1959 the benevolent Chairman allowed him to return to Beijing where he could live a modest life in a government-sponsored hotel. The juvenile emperor was now in his fifties and wisely voiced support for the Communist Party. He went on to work in the Beijing Botanical Gardens and as an editor in the literary department of the Chinese People's Political Consultant Conference, which is an arm of central government. He then became a member of the Conference, marking the completion of his redemption in the eyes of the Party.

His journey from little emperor to Japanese puppet, to exile, to prisoner, to committed communist is truly remarkable. Perhaps most astonishing is that he managed to survive all the upheaval and hardship to die of cancer, aged sixty-one. Even during the Cultural Revolution when the Red Guard were purging China's intelligentsia, the over-educated Puyi was protected by local police in 1966.

His ashes can be found with his dynastic ancestors at the Western Qing tombs outside Beijing. Puyi was the last of the Qing Dynasty which ruled from 1644 to 1911. China has had over a dozen dynasties, with some lasting for centuries while others barely survived fifteen years. Before the Qing, there was the Ming from 1368 to 1644. Emperors from both lines made the Forbidden City their home.

I leave the tiny Puyi shrine and make a beeline for the main ticket office. Tens of beggars lie in the shade of a terracotta-coloured wall. Many are amputees and most look emaciated. A uniformed guard who has just jumped out of a small police buggy is urging them to move on. Most do as they are told, hobbling back into the baking sun, asking visitors for donations as they do so. A petite girl with severe burns from head to toe remains motionless lying on a stretcher. She doesn't even flinch when flies land on her face. She might be dead. The policeman decides against forcing her to move, but is equally unconcerned about her well-being as he jumps back into his little Fisher-Price buggy and whizzes away.

Tickets for the Forbidden City cost 40 kuai but it would be a false economy not to shell out an extra 60 kuai on the audio guide. I pop in the earphones and walk through the gate. The guide automatically works out where in the vast compound you are and delivers the corresponding description of the area, describing what used to take place there in centuries past. Alas, it's a little hit and miss when it comes to giving you the information you want when you want it. Part of the problem is that the recommended route is blocked by several stories of scaffolding. The Hall of Supreme Harmony – which I'm sure is fascinating – is closed for renovation. Instead of walking through it, visitors are currently walking around it. The Hall was used for special occasions, like the Emperor's birthday and coronations, but I'll have to come back in a few months if I want to see the ornate Dragon Throne or decorative ceilings described in the brochure. Looking at what lies ahead, there seems to be as much re-construction work in the Forbidden City as can be found in Beijing's high-rising neighbourhoods. Many of the ancient compound's finest features are off limits.

For 500 years the entire Forbidden City was closed to all but a select few. Members of the Dynastic families, their servants and concubines, military leaders and the very occasional guest had the privilege of walking along the cobbles on which hundreds of thousands of tourists now traipse every year. Military and clothing exhibitions are among the main attractions but I'm a little disappointed to find myself separated from the Ming and Qing living quarters by panes of misty glass. I had hoped for something like the Palace of Versailles just outside Paris where there's only a velvet rope between tourists and well-preserved palatial bedrooms. In the Forbidden City, tourists spend much of their time outdoors, wandering down narrow old lanes between courtyards. Some of the old treasures have been plundered over the centuries, leaving the buildings as the main sightseeing attractions. Luckily, they are worth the admission fee by themselves.

Roaming around the old complex in the sun can be a draining experience so the coffee shop located roughly midway through the tourist trek provides an ideal pit stop. There had, until last year, been a Starbucks tucked away in the Hall of Preserving Harmony which court officials used during the Qing Dynasty. It caused nothing but controversy from the time it opened until it eventually closed in the summer of 2007. Plonking a Starbucks outlet on a United Nations World Heritage site outraged Beijingers – as did the fact that the chain refused to sell a range of local drinks, such as tea. A Chinese television news anchor labelled the coffee giant 'a symbol of low-end US food culture', and even surveys of foreign visitors found most people would prefer if the Forbidden City were a Starbucks-free zone. The ever-expanding corporation probably didn't endear itself to local officials when its chairman said Starbucks was merely 'educating' the Chinese market about coffee. Before long, museum curators ended their forbidden love affair with the double latte.

I'm a little sorry to have missed the photo opportunity. A beacon of global capitalism in the heart of communist China's most prestigious historical site would have been something to behold.

As I sip my overpriced mineral water purchased at the authorised cafe, I'm contemplating the symbolism behind the Starbucks brouhaha. Was this China's statement that it won't swallow everything globalisation serves up; that it won't sell out its own culture? Given that the American Express logo is incongruously plastered all over the signs outside several Forbidden City palaces, it's probably fair to conclude that Beijing wants its capitalism served a la carte.

Chinese and American tourists appear to have been engaged in an undeclared battle to see who can take the most photographs. The Americans want to be in every shot, while the Chinese are happy to swiftly photograph the sites and their accompanying blurb before moving on with military efficiency. They can enjoy it all later, but for now they want to get in and get out without missing a thing. The exceptions to this are the younger Chinese visitors who never pass up an opportunity to strike a pose. Peace signs, thumbs up, and pointing at nothing in particular are among their favourites. As usual, I've managed to forget my camera so I'll have to rely on my own memory to capture the image of a historic palace encased in scaffold.

A day in the Forbidden City is exhausting. By the time I've been through countless courtyards, half a dozen huge halls, ambled through the gardens, and visited the intriguing exhibition on concubines I'm ready to leave the hordes behind.

Outside the gate to the Forbidden City, the burns victim on the stretcher has moved about thirty feet. She's alive but alone. There is a sense of community between the other beggars who share whatever spare change and recyclable plastic comes their way. The girl on the stretcher appears to be ostracised from this group of outsiders. Tourists, including me, turn away rather than look at her disfigured face and feet. Chinese society has not traditionally been sympathetic to people with disabilities but the government is pushing a more progressive agenda in recent years. State television has run news stories on how the work of disabled artists contributes to society and the 2007 Special Olympics went some way to shifting attitudes to intellectual disabilities. The government says it wants to see greater support for people on the margins but there's not much evidence of this kind of thinking catching on outside the Forbidden City this evening. Of course, I've contributed precisely nothing to ameliorate the suffering of the girl on the stretcher. I give an empty bottle to a thin woman gnawing on a corn cob, and go in search of dinner.

I think I'm being followed. I'm headed towards the Qianhai Lake area which boasts scores of bars and restaurants, as well as a pedestrianised walkway and attractive waterside views. Walking north along the outside of the Forbidden City's west perimeter wall, I realise a man in fawn slacks and a short-sleeved beige shirt has been tracing my every step. I begin to get a little paranoid so I slow down to let him overtake. The plain-clothed gent reduces his pace accordingly. I pick up the speed and he does likewise. He's still there three minutes later when I get to a busy bridge and stop to pretend to take in the view. My tracker walks five metres past me before deciding that the view is indeed well worth pausing to appreciate. What is he playing at? I'm really not worth following. I was only joking about stirring up political unrest at the university. I'm all talk.

Despite initially thinking I was losing my mind, I'm now convinced he must be tailing me but I can't imagine why. If he really is an undercover agent, he clearly doesn't care how obvious his presence is. Maybe the Beijing authorities tell agents to randomly walk behind foreigners to keep them on their toes; or perhaps they single out those who spend too long staring into space thinking about Tiananmen Square and the Forbidden City.

I walk a little further up the road and hide behind a huge sheet of corrugated iron where several construction workers are enjoying a flask of tea. This is ridiculous on so many levels. If they follow people at random to see how they react, I'm sure lurking behind iron fences makes it look like I've got something to hide. And if I'm serious about escaping, I'd better work out a more sophisticated strategy than cowering behind a metal fence. My plain-clothed stalker never reappears and I have no satisfactory explanation for what his game was or why he stopped playing it when he did. I've been carrying a fresh bottle of water but he was hardly tracing my steps waiting for me to finish so he could recycle the plastic.

The streets surrounding the Forbidden City are busy with new black cars, all of which, I have now decided, belong to the secret service. Nowhere is there such a high concentration of identical saloons with blacked-out windows. Several restaurants along the route to Qianhai Lake have a fleet of these cars parked outside. It's probably a Party hangout. Sounds intriguing but it would look suspicious if I press my nose against the window to spy on communists so I put my head down and go looking for dinner.

I'm slightly unnerved by the earlier low-speed pursuit but my hunger is helping me focus on more pressing matters. My map suggests I take what looks like a lengthy, convoluted route to the lakefront but, in keeping with my habit of second-guessing maps – and duly getting lost – I decide to take a shortcut down an ageing alleyway. I've yet to feel threatened in Beijing so have no qualms about venturing into the crumbling neighbourhood hutong.

Beijing's hutongs are the real deal. Tiananmen is for tourists, Wangfujing is for the middle class shopaholics but the city's narrow networks of local laneways offer a glimpse of how ordinary people have lived since the thirteenth century. Many of the oldest houses are falling down. Others have been demolished and replaced. Some of the new buildings are modern but others attempt to capture the traditional hutong style of four rectangular houses arranged around a square courtyard in the middle. Despite efforts to preserve this way of life, Beijing's historic hutongs are disappearing fast so it's a shortcut I feel privileged to take.

An Italian man with a young Chinese woman trundle by in the back of a pedicab which bumps along the uneven surface of the alley. I'm tut-tutting at how they brazenly stare into people's homes as they pass, until I realise that it's an irresistibly alluring pastime. The houses are tiny and dark and residents seem content to cook outdoors, at least during the warm summer months. People here don't look like their comrades on Wangfujing Street. They seem broadly untouched by China's economic miracle, except for the fact that snooping foreigners have been poking their big noses into their homes in recent years.

I emerge from the hutong onto a traffic-jammed road and cross the street in search of food along the pedestrianised strip. The lively lakefront offers up a variety of Chinese cuisine, as well as a number of pricey bars packed with tourists. I'm getting a little sick of gloopy Chinese dishes so I sit myself down in a busy Muslim restaurant run by Uighur people.

There are at least 20 million Muslims in China, roughly seven million of whom identify themselves as belonging to the Uighur people from China's western Xinjiang province. They could hardly be less Chinese. Their autonomous region borders Kazakhstan, Tajikistan, Kyrgyzstan, Afghanistan, Pakistan, India, Mongolia and Russia, and their language is closer to Turkish than Chinese. Uighurs sound and look more like their middle Asian cousins than China's Han ethnic majority. Relations between Uighur people and the Beijing government have been regularly strained since communism swept to power in 1949. These days Beijing is attempting to foster better relations with its minority peoples but that can conflict with fears over Islamic terrorism and independence movements in Xinjiang. Central government wants to clamp down on the 'three evils' of terrorism, separatism and extremism but Uighur people say China has used the War on Terror to persecute its population without incurring disapproval from Washington.

All of that is entirely incidental to me for the moment as I examine what other diners are eating. On a table next to me a family is watching several dishes go cold. There's a heap of spicy roast mutton, some boiled vegetables, peppered chicken and what looks like naan bread. They appear to be awaiting the arrival of a family member who is holding up the show. The father is resting his forehead on the table with his eyes open, while the teenage son slouches deep into his seat reading a book. The mother is busily fixing her daughter's collar, just for the want of something to do. Nobody is eating or talking.

I order some mutton and bread and continue to observe the dysfunctional family. More food arrives but the missing family member does not. My meal is delicious. It's spicy but it's a different kind of tang to the tear-inducing flavour of Szechuan spices. I could make a habit of this.

Just as I'm polishing off my naan bread, the hitherto absent sibling arrives in a fluster for the family dinner. He is in his late twenties and accompanied by his wife who's wheeling a toddler in a buggy. Reading their apologetic gestures, I gather the young couple are blaming their son for the holdup. The child is eating a stick of processed meat and shouting at his mother. He's demanding to be unleashed from the straps of his pushchair. And he gets his way. Despite a vain attempt by the child's father to get him to stay still, the little menace grabs a messy handful of food and spins off to do a lap of the restaurant. His parents look a little uncomfortable, but are not as embarrassed as they ought to be.

I pay up and head for the door before the out of control child comes near me with his oily hands. As I leave, junior is helping himself to food from another couple's table. The couple don't look impressed and this has the potential to cause serious friction if he's not reined in.

The moral of the story is not to give too much power to a Little Emperor or all hell could break loose.

On the subway back to my new home, I try to assess what progress I've made in my effort to become a Beijinger. It's tricky because today I was playing the tourist. Whatever about the feasibility of fitting in as a resident of any major city in the globalised world, sightseeing has become foolproof for English speakers willing to cough up for an audio guide. But that doesn't really help me feel part of the real Beijing. My wander through the hutong was a peek at authentic Beijing life but I could never live there; I couldn't be a part of that.

At home in Dublin when I was daydreaming of World Citizenship, I had made the false assumption that all modern capital cities could offer similarly high standards of living. I was thinking of Paris or London or Lisbon. Even Melbourne or Auckland would clock up air miles but are still culturally familiar. It's clear now that I've made a fundamentally flawed extrapolation.

As I turn the key in the door of our new pad, I'm relieved not to be in the old dorm room and that our bed is marginally softer than rock. Now that I've a place to call home it might make it easier to settle in.

Thus far, I've become best acquainted with the western side of Beijing as well as the city's central tourist traps. Next week I'm sampling life in the expat haven of the capital's east side. Perhaps I could feel at home there if it looks a little less Chinese and a lot more international.

I move the goalposts a little every time I mull over whether integrating in China is possible. The prospect of speaking fluent Chinese and assimilating local customs currently seems remote, so I'll now consider the quest a success if I feel at home surrounded by foreigners eating hamburgers and skulling pints of Carlsberg.

It's a bit of a cop-out but it's better than admitting that I'm not the worldly free spirit I'd thought.

7

Expat Paradise

The sudden drop in temperature that accompanies the arrival of October in Beijing is more than welcome. I haven't managed to find decent antiperspirant since arriving, so the moderate temperatures are probably a relief to all around. Asian people simply don't sweat like other races. They have fewer of the apocrine glands that produce what is politely dubbed 'body odour' in the West. That's why my local supermarket doesn't bother stocking deodorant. And it's why other passengers give me a wide berth on the subway.

The chill in the air means adults are now wearing long sleeves and toddlers are no longer dressed in the conveniently aerated trousers that are common during the summer months. Rather than wear nappies, most kids in Beijing have a slice cut through the arse of their pants, facilitating casual toilet breaks. It's not uncommon to see parents pick up their little darlings in the middle of the street so junior can urinate on the kerb. Chinese people may have been blessed with odourless armpits but the whiff of fresh piss rolling down the road on a scorching summer afternoon is the same the world over. On that score, we really are all the same.

The open-backed pants look liberating for children but adults have to be careful when they've got an excitable two-year-old seated on their lap. The only thing standing between parents and a pee-soaked leg is the untrained sphincter of a toddler.

It's ten degrees celsius this evening as I arrive in Chaoyang on Beijing's east side in search of a little taste of the West. The weather feels familiar and I'm immediately struck by the skyscraping hotels and office towers that greet me at the exit of the Dongsishitiao subway station. This is more like the modern metropolis I had expected. There are plenty of foreigners around but they are a different breed to the dawdling tourists you find in Tiananmen Square. Out here, westerners are living, working and socialising – and the locals barely bat an eyelid, let alone bother to stare.

There are about 60,000 expats in Beijing and the number grows by the month as China continues to attract new foreign business. The Chaoyang district plays host to the majority of foreign residents who support scores of bars and restaurants. If you want to find a pub that shows European football and doesn't close at 11.00 pm, this is the place to look. It's easy to see why the expat community gravitates towards the east side of town. It's close to Beijing International Airport, it is the location of the leafy embassy district, and it's the only place you can get decent pizza.

Prior to the 1990s, foreigners had to stay in government-approved hotels. This made it easy to keep an eye on what was then quite a small coterie of diplomats, foreign journalists and businesspeople. There was a dearth of high standard housing in Beijing at the time but that situation has since been addressed. Unfortunately, it led to upmarket ghettos springing up across the capital's eastern neighbourhoods. Exclusive gated compounds were the only option for foreigners until 2002 when the government dropped the requirement for non-Chinese residents to live in approved housing. These days, expats can live wherever they like but many still choose the secluded apartment complexes. Compound dwellers can get by with only the rarest contact with locals. Apart from a friendly nod to the Chinese doorman guarding the electronic gates, Chaoyang foreign residents can eat in western restaurants, work in international companies, shop in specialist expat shops and surround themselves with non-Chinese neighbours.

Although I'm more than ready to rediscover pub culture and feast on what the Chinese refer to as foreign food, the gated compounds hold little appeal. They are probably best suited to those who would rather not be in Beijing in the first place.

The best thing about the expat apartment blocks is that they can get satellite TV. The government doesn't want the local Chinese exposed to the global perspective that international news channels offer, so satellite dishes are limited to buildings occupied by foreigners. Even Hong Kong-based channels are banned. Overseas stations like CNN and HBO are available in upmarket hotels but local people face stern penalties if they install an illegal dish. The Communist Party doesn't want to hear American and European do-gooders harping on about human rights and faulty Chinese goods. Worse still, opening up to foreign media would make it mighty difficult to keep a lid on what happened in Tiananmen Square in 1989. And the Chinese might find outsiders don't share their rosy view of the heroic Chairman Mao.

Taxis are cheap in Beijing. The meter starts at 10 kuai and rolls up so slowly that most short hops usually cost less than 20 kuai. If it were any colder I'd take a cab from the subway stop to the restaurant, but I feel like a stroll this evening. I walk past a group of women in their sixties dancing a slow, graceful dance around a ghetto blaster. Some are holding fans, others are pretending to. They seem more concerned with exercise than sticking strictly to the steps. Twenty metres further on, in a large paved square, dozens of couples are doing the tango to the incongruous beat of wailing Chinese music. I'm not about to join in but I do feel like pairing off the two frowning old men who are separately shuffling around the periphery attempting to perfect the moves.

I'm bound for the Kro's Nest bar and restaurant just outside Workers Stadium, the home of the Beijing Hyundai soccer team.

Despite its large neon name sign, the entrance to the Kro's Nest is not easy to find. I pass Vic's night club where well-off Chinese youngsters and expats throw their hands in the air like they just don't care, while in-house DJs pump out American hip hop music. I scan the menu of the Australian themed Outback Steakhouse next door, drooling over the prospect of a cholesterol-laden burger, and walk around the back of the building to a dark gravelly laneway which turns out to be the way into the Kro's Nest. It's a large two-storey building with stone walls and dark wooden furniture. It seems quiet for a Saturday night but it is still only 8.00 pm so the night is young.

I meet my newest friends, Martin and Cheng Cheng, and we take one of the booths upstairs. I've never met either of them before but have been put in touch with Martin through an old workmate. Everybody needs a Martin and Cheng Cheng. They know all you need to know to get by in Beijing. They have been here for a couple of years and between Martin's Irish perspective and Cheng Cheng's native knowledge, they pretty much have China sussed. Within a few minutes Martin and I realise that we have another half dozen friends in common, confirming Cheng Cheng's suspicions that Ireland is a tiny country where everybody is connected by no more than two degrees of separation. Martin had originally come to China to teach English but these days he works at a multinational PR firm, where I surmise that he's doing alright for himself. Cheng Cheng has started working for a top US broadcast network so, unlike most Beijingers, she has a more outward perspective on the world. I learn how to save money on public transport, what to pay for DVDs and where to buy western-strength deodorant. I only wish I'd met them sooner.

They certainly know good food. The Kro's Nest serves up giant pizzas freshly baked in the oven downstairs. Decent pizza is hard to come by in Beijing, despite a number of downtown restaurants describing themselves as pizza joints. Lesser establishments serve up frozen fare with bland cheese and crunchy bread bases in need of a dollop of tomato sauce. But the Kro's Nest knows its expat market and they whip up their own bases on site.

I'm already tiring of Chinese food so I can only imagine how people who have been here years must feel. All that monosodium glutamate can't be good. MSG is the allegedly evil flavour enhancer widely used in Chinese cooking – and in other Asian cuisine – to improve savoury food. Some people are MSG intolerant and develop the headaches, sweating and chest pain associated with Chinese Restaurant Syndrome if they eat too much. This hasn't happened to me yet – I'm just of sick of eating sticky rice with goo sauce.

This place also has Guinness on tap but I stick with the local brew. I'm not much of a connoisseur, but Guinness aficionados usually grumble about how you can't get a good pint outside Ireland. I'm sure the master brewers in St James's Gate have been improving their supersensitive stout for 250 years but if self-appointed barstool experts reckon Guinness isn't quite the same in London, then I'm not willing to try it in Beijing.

Once we've polished off a Hawaiian pizza and a few cheap pints of Yanjing beer, we pay up and make for a nearby expat hangout called The Den.

It's wall to wall Big Noses in The Den and they're charging a little over the odds for a pint. Plenty of the expats in Chaoyang are on expat salaries so the living is still cheap and easy. We join a gang that Martin knows through work. There's a bunch of Americans from the PR firm, a pair of Austrian junior diplomats, and a Korean Greenpeace activist. Everybody is speaking English. Once it's clear that I'm a relative newbie, more inside dope is dispensed while an Ireland rugby match plays in the background and I begin to feel like this is my local. Unfortunately, it's about twenty miles from where I live.

The evening follows a familiar pattern until around 1.30 am when a troop of Chinese ladies-of-the-night file in. The western men are well jarred and these ladies are making their intentions clear. It's entirely obvious what's going on but neither the bar staff nor the punters pay any mind. I'm the only one that this scene is new to.

The middle-aged Scotsman enjoying a few quiet pints at the bar watching rugby suddenly finds himself flanked by two eager young ladies competing for his attention. He's not the least bit interested but his new admirers are persistent and it takes quite a while for them to give up and move on. The younger of the two girls must be no more than eighteen and is wearing a red hooded zip-up top. The zip is open, revealing a tight t-shirt hugging her tiny figure. The wire of her AA cup push-up bra gives her a lumpy chest that would otherwise be naturally flat. She's not as au fait with the game as the older girls who are flashing smiles at all and sundry.

The Scotsman is still being harassed by the older of his two wannabe temporary girlfriends but he's clearly more in love with the rugby match and has no interest in slipping off his wedding ring – not that it would matter a great deal to the ladies I suspect. The relatively older girl to his left is in her mid-twenties and dressed for the job. Her black polyester dress hugs the curve of her belly which hangs over an unflattering red belt. She was probably pretty once. These days it seems the Saturday night routine is all too predictable for her and she surely despises having to charm clients in whom she would have no interest if the financial balance wasn't so heavily weighted against her. Her thick foundation and heavy green eye shadow are frankly frightening and her joyless smile is far from attractive but she'll probably find success before the night is out.

I rescue our Celtic cousin by leaning in to exchange my expert analysis of what's gone wrong with rugby in the northern hemisphere. I haven't a clue what I'm talking about. He appreciates the intervention and goes as far as to declare Brian O'Driscoll the greatest centre on the planet. I agree and order another tray of drinks. The Scotsman is included in the round, but the ladies are not. They move on. Time is money.

In no time at all, the older of the two is twirling the last few hairs on the head of a man at the bar who is wearing a South African rugby jersey. His initial resistance to her advances is wavering and they'll be leaving together shortly.

The younger girl is now in the arms of the well-sozzled English bloke in a salmon-coloured Ralph Lauren shirt sitting behind us. His eyelids are drooping and with any luck, so will his sexual prowess. I can't stand the thought of an overweight, permatanned drunk dragging himself on top of this young one. He looks like he's at the point in a drinking session where he is wildly over-estimating himself in every way and he'll probably wake up tomorrow morning presuming he was a stud, but remembering little about the transaction. I'm hoping they'll go back to his place, he'll pass out, she'll relieve him of 500 kuai and get home before her mother starts wondering where she is.

Prostitution aside, the romantic combination of western men and Chinese women is a common sight in Beijing. This aggravates the gender disparity caused by the one child policy – there are already too few young women in China and now some of them are taking off with foreigners. Around 70,000 couples of mixed nationalities were married in China last year. It might not seem significant given there were just shy of 10 million weddings, but the number of expats shacking up with locals has been increasing steeply. The bulk of these are foreign men taking local brides. It's rare to see a western girl with a Chinese man and, when you do, they are often roughly the same age. The pairing of ageing western men and barely legal Chinese girls is more frequent. I've yet to clap eyes on a poorly preserved 50-year-old western lady with a fit-looking 20-year-old Beijing boy on her arm. The same goes for ageing Chinese men hooking up with feisty western females. I'm sure there are plenty of people who fit that description but it's not a common sight.

I'm ready to go home so I'm not displeased to overhear a debate coming from the other end of the table about the number of taxis we'll need. Unfortunately, my hearing has been dampened by drink and I missed the fact that the discussion is on how we're going to get to the nearby Sanlitun bar street. We pay the bill and everybody hops into taxis for what turns out to be a two minute trip to the edge of the upmarket embassy area. The embassy district is exactly what I had expected: a long strip of heavily guarded high-walled buildings behind reinforced gates. But turn a corner and you're greeted by a blinding sea of neon. Bars began springing up on Sanlitun Street as the number of foreigners in the city grew. These days it's party central. At 3.00 am on a Saturday night it is packed with expats and well-to-do Chinese revellers in search of the high life.

A huge red cloth sign hangs between two trees at the bottom of the street. It reads: 'Reject drugs, cherish lives'. Clearly some Sanlitun party animals are getting a bit carried away for the liking of the authorities. Eric, one of my new drinking buddies, a Californian with a skater-dude accent, recounts the tale of a recent drug raid. A fortnight ago police descended on the street, rounding up drug dealers in a cackhanded crackdown. African drug dealers were hauled into the police station, along with any other young black men police came across. Eric claims several expats, including tourists and the son of the Grenada Ambassador, found themselves on the wrong end of police brutality. The Ambassador was not best pleased when he showed up to retrieve his son and found him in need of hospital treatment. So much for diplomatic immunity.

The other two Americans in the taxi are veteran expats and it's agreed that a blind eye has long been turned to recreational drug use on the hedonistic street. But, they sigh, the Chinese authorities can be an unpredictable force.

The same blind eye watches over prostitution in night clubs and massage parlours in Beijing, and Sanlitun Street is no exception. Most nightspots are reputable but there is a seediness to some of the bars. As our taxi slowly crawls by a string of pubs and restaurants, I can see a line of heavily made-up girls propping up a bar sipping cocktails which reminds me of the earlier scene in The Den. Even the delightfully named Pure Girl Bar doesn't look as wholesome as the name might suggest.

Resisting the temptation to stay in the taxi until it brings me home, I get out and follow my herd of new friends who appear to know where they are going. The path is packed with staggering punters and club managers urging us to sample the atmosphere in their bars. We cross the road in front of slow-moving traffic, too intoxicated to pay any heed to the car horns, and arrive at a pub – the name of which has been washed from my memory by a gallon of beer. Things get a little hazy at this point, but I recall several rounds of Jack Daniels and Coke landing on our table and at some point I climbed into a cab and settled in for the long drive home.

Despite the distance, taking a taxi to the other side of the city only costs 60 kuai. And the journey flies when you're three sheets to the wind. I may also have nodded off briefly which helped pass the time.

When I reach my destination I step out of the cab onto the usually busy street which is now deserted. It's at this point I remember that the university campus goes into lockdown at 11.00 pm. It's now 4.30 am. I had been warned about this but it just never came up until now. On the upside, things get going again around 6.00 am so I could just sit it out.

Better still, I could try to scale the gate. It's not a particularly high gate but it is awkward to climb because it is an unstable series of diagonal steel bars; there's no horizontal ledge to plant your foot on. It rattles loudly as soon as I put my hand on it, even though I'm trying not to draw attention to myself. It's like this gate is designed to be difficult to get over after a fill of pints.

Not surprisingly, I make an unmerciful racket clamouring over and then catch my foot on a bar before landing on my arse. As I painlessly hit the ground inside the campus, a bright light flicks on. Shit. I'm convinced I've been caught by the baby-faced night watchman. I stay perfectly still. No sign of security; no sound of rabid hounds baying for my blood. I dust myself off and tiptoe past the security booth where I spy a guard snoring his little head off. Good job, sonny.

However, it's not as simple as hopping over the gate and ducking past security. My apartment building is also locked up and in complete darkness. I don't have a key to the front door but there is a bell. I'm in two minds whether to ring it, but it's chilly out here and there are bats as big as dragonflies flapping overhead.

I hit the buzzer. There's no answer. I buzz again. And again. As I'm sobering up and trying to figure out what I might do with the next couple of hours if nobody lets me in, a light flickers inside the building. A grouchy doorman emerges from a room behind the reception desk with a bunch of keys in his hand. When the light comes on in the porch I can see he's wearing long johns and a surly scowl. Now might be a good time to wheel out some of the Chinese I've been learning. I give him my best efforts at sorry in Mandarin – 'dui bu qi' – but he is unmoved. I consider having another go at pronouncing it but rather than run the risk of irritating him further I offer an apologetic bow and jump in the lift.

My apartment may be in the same city as Sanlitun but it feels a million miles away. Maybe it's just because my brain is bathed in an alcohol solution but I begin to think I'm better off in this unfashionable western district than in the bright lights of Chaoyang's foreign compounds. Here, at least, it feels wholly Chinese. The same can't really be said for Sanlitun.

It's not so much that globalisation means we can live anywhere; it just means you can recreate your home lifestyle in most capital cities if you've got enough cash. Indeed, you can exist 5,000 miles from home without ever making any attempt to integrate.

The fact that Chaoyang is only a subway ride away and I can top up on a dose of western culture any time I like is reassuring. But it also emboldens me to make more effort to fit in around my west side neighbourhood. I don't want to live in Expatland. It seems pointless, unless you've been posted to Beijing against your will.

I'm attempting to figure out China and maybe learn a little about myself in the process. I won't learn much in The Den or Kro's Nest.

Although I'm definitely going back for a weekly pizza.

8

Price of Progress

My neighbourhood is growing on me – and I'm getting braver. The laneway full of grubby restaurants that frightened Girlfriend and me away just a couple of weeks ago is no longer as off-putting. They still have caterpillars on sticks and the whole place could be cleaner but tonight we're conquering our fear in the interest of integration. Anyway, it doesn't look half as filthy if you go down when it's dark.

Things have changed a little since we first ventured into the frenetic side street. A Uighur guy who used to sell roast mutton on skewers in the middle of the street has moved into a compact but newly-kitted out restaurant unit which had been dark and derelict a fortnight ago. A family with terrible teeth have begun selling fruit from the trailer on the back of a tricycle in the space where the mutton stand used to be. Apart from that, I have the impression that things have looked more or less the same here for decades. Some people have grown up living and working in the family-run restaurants and shops that line the alley. Sadly for them, there's a revolution coming.

We walk to the end to inspect all the options. Our standards are slowly dissolving into thick smoggy air but we still want to pick the most hygienic-looking place on the strip. These are the kinds of food stalls that are renowned for giving you a dodgy belly. Especially if your belly is unaccustomed to sharing food with foreign bacteria.

There's no clear winner in our search for the most sanitary restaurant in the lane, so we settle on a place serving kebabs. It's not exactly spotless but it has the advantage of offering outdoor seating. There's only one table so we pull up two seats and order some spicy lamb skewers, toasted bread and potatoes.

The owner treats us like we're old friends. He's twenty-seven but carries himself like a man twice his age, proudly pushing his pot belly out as he gives us a warm welcome. A smart sports jacket over a crisply ironed black shirt and a big-buckled belt make him look marginally better off than his clientele. The fact that he owns an iron is a bit posh around here.

He tells us his name but he giggles like a girl every time we attempt to pronounce it. His Chinese name sounds vaguely like Johnny so we suggest he adopt it for the evening. He loves it. Lots of Chinese people, especially the younger crowd, are taking on English monikers in addition to their given names. It's not unusual for somebody to introduce themselves by saying, 'My Chinese name is Hu Jingtao, but my English name is Joe'. It's handy for those of us who don't speak Mandarin, but plenty of Chinese people think it's a silly fad devised as a sop to dumb foreigners. They have a point, but Johnny seems okay with it. He gives us Chinese names but we can't pronounce those either.

The food is cooked outdoors by an affable young man wearing a whitish coat and chef's hat. I suspect both are filthy but it's too dark to tell, which is probably for the best. When the red hot skewers arrive, Johnny sits himself down at the table with a beer in his hand and signals to his underling to bring three glasses. We have already ordered two bottles of beer but a third arrives. Johnny cracks it open and tops up our glasses before filling his own. Then the young multitasking chef returns with three sealed glasses of a clear liquid with a pepper floating in each. This, we are told, is *bai jiu*. The aluminium lids are peeled off the three glasses and Johnny, Girlfriend and I clink while saying 'cheers'. But Johnny adds an enthusiastic 'gan bei!' and proceeds to knock back the contents of the glass. 'Gan bei', we guess, means you have to polish off whatever is in front of you. Fair enough, we follow suit. *Bai jiu* is a spirit that varies in strength from twenty per cent alcohol to around sixty per cent. It burns our throats off but you don't want to be rude so we offer a sham look of satisfaction. Johnny sees through our lame act and chuckles. I suspect he'd have been disappointed if we'd genuinely enjoyed it.

The lamb skewers are delicious. There are four small pieces of tender, spicy meat, as well as a lump of fat in the middle. Johnny can't believe I'm shying away from the roasted gristle which is the best part as far as he's concerned. But I eat around it. Bread doused in an oily seasoning and toasted on hot coals arrives next, along with thinly sliced potatoes which look like large crisps. It's tasty, if a little oily.

Johnny's excitement in sitting with us and the effect of the *bai jiu* help us overlook the fact that the table was dirty when we sat down and dust is swirling around the street while passersby spit freely. This is authentic China and I like it.

Johnny gets another round of drinks in and presents us with a plate of peanuts. The nuts are soaked in cold salted water but it's as close to bar snacks as we're going to get. The procession of nosey locals slows down to take a look at us as they pass. Some stop to order half a dozen lamb kebabs so they can examine us while they wait for their skewers. We're good for business.

I congratulate Johnny on running his own restaurant at the tender age of twenty-seven but he shakes his head wistfully. Business is going downhill he says. How can this be? There's more money than ever in Beijing and this alley does a roaring passing trade. Living is getting harder instead of easier for small businesses, Johnny explains.

He unpeels another pair of *bai jiu* glasses – Girlfriend is wisely counting herself out of the round at this stage – and we say 'gan bei' before Johnny adopts a more serious tone. It had been all fun and games up to this point. The trouble is that the cost of food is going through the roof but salaries for ordinary people have not kept pace. The inflation of meat prices is well into double digits, meaning running costs for restaurateurs are rocketing but customers can't tolerate price hikes. On top of that, other basic living costs like clothing, accommodation and fuel are spiralling upwards. This stifles the spending power of Johnny's customer base.

'Gan bei!' he exclaims in a bid to lift the mood, and we're now drinking beer like it's about to be rationed by the government. We're gulping from tiny glasses so it's a bit like doing shots of lager and having to refill after every swig.

The young cook has kept his distance but as the busy spell peters out, Johnny beckons him over. He's not inviting him to join us; rather the cook has been instructed to entertain. He comes back with a bowl of green vegetables. They're like pea pods but slightly larger. With a bit of salt, they make for good nibbles.

The chef is behaving a little strangely all of a sudden. He has an intense look on his face as he stares into space. He looks like he might explode at any minute. I look at Johnny to gauge his reaction but he is nodding in approval. Then, the cook picks up a bowl and stares at it while taking slow, deep breaths. In a split-second, he chops the bowl in two pieces with an unmerciful crack using only two fingers. Johnny bursts into applause, looking at us in a way that suggests we should join in. It was very impressive but I'm still a little in shock. It came out of nowhere.

But the show doesn't end there. The cook wraps a piece of wire around his torso three times and ties it at the front. He's smiling as he does it and chatting to Johnny. Then, just as suddenly as before, his face goes red and he flexes his chest causing the wires to

91

snap. We clap – it's excellent street theatre. Oh God, now he's getting the bricks.

I hadn't been sure why, but there's a pile of new-looking red bricks stacked behind the table. I now suspect they might be purely for the purpose of dazzling foreign guests. The cook does his usual build-up – his red face shakes like he's constipated – before smashing the brick in halves with predictably impressive intensity. He takes the applause, gives a quick bow and adds new coals to the fires at Johnny's suggestion.

Business isn't booming but there's a steady flow of people through the alley. Even if living is getting more expensive, eating here is still far cheaper than buying food in the supermarket. In any case, profit doesn't even seem to be the aim of the game for most of the enterprises around here. These are overstaffed family-run shops and restaurants. It's a community, a way of life. Young entrepreneurs like Johnny would like to turn a profit but even he employs his aunt and uncle. They have very little to do other than chew the fat with a neighbouring shopkeeper. Employment is a social good.

Everybody knows everything about everybody around here and there's no shortage of gossip. Johnny tells us, with a straight face, that his local rival in the kebab business doesn't use real lamb.

'That guy brushes other meats with a dark seasoning oil and passes it off as fresh lamb,' he tells us solemnly.

I suspect savvy locals would suss that out in a flash but decide against pulling him up on it, especially because he's opening a new bottle of beer.

His tongue has been loosened by the booze so Johnny takes a quick look around before confiding that he's looking to sell up. I ask him why he wants to leave and why it's such a secret. It turns out he wants to offload the business before it becomes public knowledge that the whole place is to change forever next year.

The government has approached Johnny and told him his restaurant and all the shops on one side of the lane are to be replaced with a new hotel. That's progress for you. Only one side is affected but the community atmosphere on the whole street will be finished once construction work starts. Business owners will be compensated but there is no option but to move out and watch the bulldozers move in. In a couple of years, a government-owned high-rise five-star hotel will stand where Johnny's restaurant and kebab stall is now.

I commiserate and appreciate being taken into his confidence.

Just then the cook arrives with more unordered snacks. They really know how to look after guests but the bonus grub isn't exactly up my street. However, it would be terminally rude to turn our noses up at Johnny's hospitality, especially now that we're all such good pals.

Roasted cow tendon is first. It's hard and chewy but has been doused in the same spicy sauce as the lamb we ate earlier. So I dig in like a good guest should. I'm relieved once I've managed to swallow it, washing it down with a little more beer. Let's hope it stays down.

The cook immediately presents us with a plate of kebabs. Johnny says it's chicken but it doesn't look like it. I have a nibble. It's all skin and bone. What part of the chicken? I ask. Johnny's mouth is full so he points to his throat. That makes sense – we're eating chicken neck. Well, he is. Girlfriend and I can't stomach it so we politely decline.

Johnny is determined to be a good host and leave a lasting impression on his new foreign friends. So he has one final delicacy in store: roasted caterpillar in its own cocoon. We've already used up our Get Out of Eating Weird Shit pass and can't very well snub him twice in a row. The beer and spirit combo is powerful stuff so we're ready for anything. He brings us five caterpillars on a skewer and sniggers up his sleeve as he sees the look on our faces.

'Just one, just one,' he says. We bargain him down to letting us off the hook if we eat one between two of us. He agrees. His aunt and uncle have arrived to see what all the fuss is about. The uncle looks the spitting image of Mel Brooks but I'm ninety-nine per cent sure it's not him. The aunt is wearing an apron to give the impression that she is somehow involved in food preparation but the pair of them are in charge of social networking as far as I can see.

I bite through the crunchy cocoon which has been roasted into a thin crispy shell. The meat inside isn't too bad. It's soft and chewy and tastes like tender chicken. It's juicy, which would be alright if we could forget what we're eating. But neither of us can get over the psychological hurdle presented by ingesting a caterpillar. We swallow as quickly as possible and the small crowd claps and laughs at the show we've reluctantly put on. To my mind, it wasn't as impressive as smashing a brick with your finger tips but it has the same effect.

I can't believe I ate a caterpillar. So much unrealised potential.

It's time to go. If we stick around they'll keep feeding us strange snacks and Johnny has just told us that he has recently enjoyed a plate of cow penis. Better go before he serves up cat testicles or some such. The bill comes to just shy of 50 kuai even though we've been eating and drinking all night. One beer could easily set you back 50 kuai in a European capital – although you wouldn't be sitting at a dirty table down a dark alley. Johnny says the extra food and all those glasses of *bai jiu* spirit are on the house because we're friends now. No wonder he hasn't made his first million yet. He insists we come back next week and we agree on the condition that we don't have to swallow insects.

Even two days after Friday night at Johnny's Place, I'm feeling a little ropey. Yesterday was a write off. I could blame the bugs and the cow tendon but it was probably the booze. We have some more wholesome entertainment pencilled in tonight. It's the Mid-

Autumn Festival and there has been great activity in local parks preparing celebrations.

Today is also called Moon Day as it occurs on the autumn equinox. All week there have been elaborate displays of moon cakes in the supermarkets and on makeshift street stalls. Moon cakes are round-shaped baked desserts which are a little like western fruit cakes. They can also have sesame seeds, nuts and red beans, and often feature an egg yolk in the centre. I'm not a big fan, but the Chinese go wild for them.

Legend has it that when the Mongolians ruled China in the fourteenth century, disgruntled leaders from the overthrown Sung Dynasty ordered the baking of special cakes to mark the equinox. Baked into each cake was a plan to attack the Mongolians. The story goes that the Chinese overthrew their government based on this tasty strategy and have celebrated with moon cakes ever since. If the ones I've eaten are anything to go by, they may still be throwing some battle blueprints into the mix for old times' sake. I'm sure I still taste the ink. As a rule, the Chinese are not particularly good at cake.

There's a crowd of people outside a ticket booth at the entrance to the park. They are forming what should be a queue but is, in fact, just a melee. Everybody is battling to get tickets into the serene park so they can celebrate the family festival in peace with their loved ones. But before the calm, it's a storm of pushing and shoving.

Queuing can be a nightmare in China. At the beginning, I was far too polite, and naively expected that the basic standards of decency and manners might apply. Some values are universal, surely. A few elbows in the ribs put paid to that notion.

At train stations, or even getting into lifts, people will emerge out of nowhere just to jump in front of you. Most people wait their turn to buy subway tickets but there's always some chancer slinking in from the side to slide his money towards the cashier. They

don't care if you mete out a frosty-nosed stare as they scurry off –
Lord knows I've tried. I'm very slowly learning to use a broad
stance and pointy elbows as a deterrent to queue skippers.

Getting tickets for the park tonight is like trying to get into the
front row at a rock concert. Eventually, after swaying back and
forth with the crowd for twenty minutes, being jostled and stepped
on, I get a couple of tickets. And they're not cheap. It's 30 kuai a
head tonight – not an insubstantial sum for a family event. It's a
good job nobody has large families.

Inside the park there's a large dark green canvas partition surrounding an inner arena where the entertainment will take place.
Locals with residents' permits can get into the perimeter area
around the arena but only ticket-holders have access to the show.
Scores of people are gathered around the entrance to the exclusive
inner section of the park. Some are pressing their faces against the
partition in the hope of seeing what's so great that it costs 30 kuai
a ticket.

There's a large paper dragon moving like a wave while primi-
tive fireworks spark overhead. The dragon is controlled by ten
young men wearing red pyjama bottoms and a red cloth tied
around their forehead. To make the fireworks, clumps of iron fil-
ings are put into a furnace and removed while they are red hot.
The searing ball of iron dust is then batted into the air with a
wooden paddle, producing a short-lived but spectacular splash of
light. The crowd inside love it, but their yelps must make those
outside the exclusion zone wish they could be part of the action.

Unfortunately, that's about as good as it gets. We follow the
noise to the far end of the park where a terrible troupe of cabaret
singers is belting out crowd favourites in time with a blaring backing tape. When I say 'crowd', I'm only referring to around 100
people.

One of the three entertainers is a crazy looking lady in her fifties who wails and warbles so far out of tune that the small audi-

ence are covering their ears. Some punters try to get as far away as possible – children are crying – but others are so bemused that they just plug their ears and keep their eyes on this phenomenally awful shrieking lady. She must be the wife of a Party official because it's not popular demand that has won her the right to sing her top ten favourite show tunes at the Mid-Autumn Festival.

She is followed by what I'm guessing is a washed up balladeer. He used to be somebody but his star faded. The dye in his thinning hair is unconvincing and he moves across the tiny stage with a confidence that suggests he has played bigger venues than this. He has the swagger of an old pro but his voice is as weak as the audience response. However, once his mushy love song has reached a deafening crescendo and his big finish is met with a ripple of underwhelmed applause, I'm calling for an encore. It's not that he's won me over, but I can see the wailing woman limbering up for a second shot at the title of World's Worst Warbler. Let's go for a walk.

There isn't much of an atmosphere at the festival, probably because there are more people in the small space outside the canvas partition than there are enjoying the show inside. Most local people simply can't afford the admission fee.

The excitement is getting too much for some of those who have their faces pressed against the canvas and they are now trying to pull down the hoarding just far enough so they can catch a glimpse of the mysterious show. If only they knew how little they were missing. I want to leave and I've only been here forty-five minutes.

Hang on, things are about to get interesting. The hoarding has been breached. Brilliant! A forty-five-year-old rotund woman has ripped a two foot gap at the bottom of the canvas and has crawled through. She's followed by a twelve-year-old girl and her granny. Two teenage boys squeeze through next. Anyone who manages to get in is sprinting as though their lives depend on it. It's vital that they mix in with the crowd so they can't be picked out and evicted.

A stream of twenty or so people barge through the gap before the security kids even notice. It's every man, woman and child for themselves once you're in.

Such is the mix of elation and anxiety on their faces you'd think they were escaping from a prison camp. But these people are desperate to get in rather than get out. They need to escape the excruciatingly dull life on the outside and make it to the Promised Land inside. Families will be separated; children may be left outside crying for their parents but this show is not to be missed. Or so they think.

Three young guards run over shouting and gesturing with all the authority of a six-year-old dressed up as a cop for Halloween. A few bigger boys in uniforms arrive and radio for reinforcements. They guard the gap as though it's the perimeter wall outside the Forbidden City, and the stream of rogue punters is stemmed for now.

The price of tickets to low grade local entertainment, on top of the surging costs of food and clothing that concerned Johnny, is a worry. China is getting rich quick, but the gap between the well-heeled, affluent business class and the hard-up proletariat is growing. Much of the debate on poverty here centres on the disparity between standards of living in the countryside and those living in cities. But the struggling farmers and urban workers have a lot in common: neither group can take full part in the country's economic miracle.

Spreading the fruits of success around isn't just a matter of doing the decent thing or being true to the Party's communist roots, it's the key to long-term stability. No government would want to face an uprising of peasant farmers and factory workers but it would be unthinkable for the Chinese Communist Party. This is a movement that won power on the back of promises to end inequality and make rural workers their heroes.

Rural communities have been decimated by the migration of its youth to urban centres as the mass production line replaces agriculture. Farm life is under threat so the government is making all the right noises about pursuing 'balanced development' and offering more support to poor villagers.

Through grants and aid, Beijing leaders hope discontent in the countryside can be killed with kindness. But if that doesn't work, the Communist Party could be confronted with a grassroots socialist revolution. Most people here don't know what happened the last time protesters assembled in central Beijing to express discontent with their government.

It might take time, but it's not unthinkable to imagine Chinese people getting worked up at the growing gulf between rich and poor. It is a little galling that Party officials and business bigwigs are eating New Zealand steaks in posh restaurants while ordinary people are struggling to afford a half dozen roasted caterpillars.

9

War on Weather

Am I the only one who isn't wearing a face mask today? Cyclists here don't bother with helmets, reflective jackets or lights on their bikes but they have the good sense to sport surgical masks when the pollution is particularly heavy.

The city looks like a scene from a news report on the SARS or bird flu outbreaks. But Beijingers are not protecting themselves from a virulent virus; it's the filthy atmosphere that's threatening public health. Pedestrians too can be seen covering their mouths this morning as they make their way through the heaviest smog I've seen here – or anywhere – to date.

The authorities like to cloud the air with talk of more official 'blue days' and claims that the situation is not as bad as it used to be, but there's no escaping the bald facts. Beijing is a pollution black spot.

Inhaling exhaust fumes all day every day in a smoggy city wipes a full thirty years off your life. Traffic police in China have a life expectancy of just forty-three years. They're middle-aged on their twenty-first birthday. Cops who spend their days directing Beijing's gridlock must have to lie on life insurance forms. If I were them I'd pretend to work for the bomb squad or to be a north Atlantic crab fisherman. You know – something safe.

I'm en route to a bakery I've heard about which purports to sell French bread. It even has a Frenchy name so I'm hoping for bona fide baguettes. Getting your mitts on a decent batch loaf or bread roll in Beijing is not easy. My local supermarket has a whole section set aside for gourmet breads, in addition to several shelves of cheapo sliced pans. The trouble is that it is all saturated with sugar. It just won't do when you've a hankering for a savoury sandwich.

It's the bones of a mile to the next major junction where I'm hoping to find *une vrai boulangerie* so there's plenty of time to inhale gallons of nitrogen dioxide, carbon monoxide and whatever other poisons are now nestling in my lungs. I'm beginning to wish I'd stayed indoors. Maybe the standard soft, sweet bread isn't so bad with jam. I'm just being greedy by wishing for a crunchy crust.

The Chinese have gone wild for bread lately. Traditional steamed buns still rule the roost but discerning consumers are keeping my local street's two identical bakeries in business. But Beijing bakers tend to treat breads as an extension of the cake family so whether it's shaped like a croissant, a Vienna roll or a lump of turnover, it tastes like either brioche or Madeira.

Pollution crept towards the top of the political agenda in July 2001 after Beijing's successful bid to host the 2008 Olympics. However, despite the best of intentions, planners have struggled to clear the air. The number of private cars has trebled since then, and my own spluttering lungs tell me it's a nut they have yet to crack. But it's not for the want of trying.

The government accepts that carbon emissions from heavy industry are an important piece of the puzzle but it would take something dramatic to make a dent in the giant blanket of smog that covers the city. Luckily, there are some things you can do in a single party political system that might not play so well with focus groups in a western democracy.

The government decreed that hundreds of factories would simply be turned off ahead of the Olympics – only to be turned on again when the show is over. Workers would be told to come back in a few months once the world's cameras are pointed in another direction.

Other factory staff were luckier still. Their plants were moved, relocated to out-of-the-way provinces where they can smoke like chimneys, miles from the Beijing skyline.

The government doesn't have to worry so much about losing a local election or facing protests in Tiananmen Square from angry workers. That's not to say factory workers were happy about being uprooted. It's just that they might have kicked up more of a fuss if they were, say, French.

Despite not doing a whole lot about pollution until they got the Olympics – because curbing fossil fuel emissions would only hamper China's exponential industrial development – Beijing officialdom suddenly focused its collective mind on smashing smog when the International Olympic Committee began warning that events like the marathon would have to be rescheduled for health reasons.

So, a multimillion dollar budget was thrown at the hilariously titled Weather Modification Office.

Scientists at the WMO attempt to make rain by firing small chemical bombs at clouds. Using rocket-launchers and anti-aircraft guns, they fire silver iodide pellets into the sky hoping to make clouds heavy enough to induce a downpour.

The heavily armed weathermen are better equipped than the military forces of a small country. In centres across China, they have 7,100 anti-aircraft guns, 4,991 specially-adapted rocket launchers and over 30 aeroplanes at their disposal. Meteorologists here seem as hawkish as American neo-conservatives. As far as they are concerned, clouds entering Beijing's airspace represent a clear and present danger. The boffins demand pre-emptive strikes against the Cirrostratus of Evil to disable their weapons of mass disruption.

Between smog and storms, nature is an awful inconvenience. The weather warriors plan to show off their rain-making skills by making it rain the day before the Olympic opening ceremony. This, they say, will protect against a cloudburst on the first day of the Games and improve the atmosphere ahead of major outdoor events. There's plenty of scepticism about whether or not this is any more effective than performing a mass rain dance up and down Wangfujing Street but try telling that to the Chinese.

I humbly asked a Chinese colleague yesterday whether it might have been better to build a retractable roof for the spectacular Olympic Stadium, affectionately known locally as the Bird's Nest. That, I was informed tersely, would have been very expensive. Firing cannons at clouds must be cheap I suppose.

Pollution and rain haven't been the only target for Beijing's weathermen; they also want to control sandstorms and have embarked on colossal tree-planting projects in the capital's hinterland. The big idea is to have a huge shelter belt north of Beijing to act as a buffer against all the pesky sand that usually comes down from Mongolia. It's like the Great Wall only greener.

So, even if the wind blows tonnes of sand in the direction of the Olympic stadium, it won't matter. Apart from the sandpit at the long jump, there shouldn't be a stray grain of silica to be found in the city.

The manic preparations for the Olympics spawned plenty of other wacky initiatives that would be laughed off the political stage in most countries. Like any good marketeers, Beijing did a little research before charging headlong into its Olympic planning.

They asked a gang of big-nosed visitors what they like, really liked and loved about Beijing. Unfortunately, these bloody foreigners weren't attuned to how surveys are answered here in the People's Republic. Some of them voiced concerns, complaints even. Cheeky pups.

It turns out tourists thought Beijing was a tad smoggy. And it can be tricky to navigate. And some of the signs are only in Chinese script. And it's hard to find somebody with a decent grasp of English. Oh and Beijingers have a nasty habit of spitting in the street. And they aren't friendly enough. Could they smile a bit more? And they aren't great at queuing.

Oh dear. Perhaps a little taken aback, the Chinese government resisted saying, 'Well, excuse us. Sorry we asked', and decided to look at how they could solve the problems aired by the picky, pampered Westerners.

Of course, the best way to develop radical new policies is to set up committees – loads of them.

The Spiritual Civilisation Office is a crack squad of Party bureaucrats charged with westernising people's manners and increasing the number of English speakers. Their job is to hit the entirely arbitrary target of making thirty-five per cent of the city's population competent in English. There's no need to define linguistic competency; that'd over-complicate matters. The project will be a success if the committee deems it to be so.

Taxi drivers faced mandatory English lessons, and classes in 'Olympic English' sprang up across the city. Stock phrases like 'Welcome to China' and 'We are ready' have been pushed by organisers.

However, efforts to tackle spitting have been an unqualified failure as far as I'm concerned. There were promises to put up signs warning people not to spit on penalty of heavy fines. But not a day goes by without the sight of a wizened old-timer hocking up a big greener and gullying it onto the path. They don't look too fearful of the supposedly dreaded fines. Even if the authorities could wipe out spitting on public transport it would be a marked improvement but success has been limited there too. Some people still spit in the aisle of public buses. Have they learned nothing from SARS?

The apparent inability of Beijingers to queue is also under the microscope. That might seem like a tricky one to solve. It requires deep social and cultural change; the undoing of generations of queue skipping. But the committee in charge of good manners has a simple response: They launched Voluntary Wait in Line Day.

Since the beginning of 2007, the eleventh day of every month has seen a special push to make the city more civilised. You see uniformed queuing monitors with red flags and whistles standing at bus stops literally keeping people in line.

'It's civilised to queue, it's glorious to be polite.' The slogan is part of a campaign to convince Chinese people that they will bring shame on their country if foreigners are upset by their reluctance to form orderly queues. They care what people think around here.

To measure their success, researchers at the Renmin University of China have drawn up a 'Civic Index' to measure public etiquette levels. Every few weeks they issue a report on how things are progressing and, unsurprisingly, the index has been rising steadily. Well done everybody.

Quashing spitting and penalising queue jumpers are all very well but there is a danger that the Mandarin mandarins could antagonise locals by forcing them to become westernised. Some measures designed to improve tourists' impression of Beijing surely go too far.

The first time I went to the US, I found it quite hilarious that stores pay 'greeters' to welcome you to their shop. In fairness, they get good value out of them by making them say 'goodbye, have a nice day' as you leave, but I still couldn't help but feel that it was a waste of money. If the shop is employing people to do virtually nothing, it probably adds to the price of the tat on sale inside. Given the choice, I bet most people would opt not to pay to be welcomed to a shoe shop.

Unfortunately, it's a craze that's starting to catch on in Europe, but I thought the Chinese would be too savvy for that kind of American faux friendliness.

So it's the Yanks that I blame for China's most hilarious effort to make foreigners feel at home: They have recruited smilers. Can you guess what their job is? That's right, these volunteers stroll around the streets smiling at people and offering help to foreign tourists. Most of them are students keen to practice their English and be a part of the Olympics excitement. But they don't just beam at people who have three chins and wear cameras around their necks, they smile at everybody. The aim is to improve the general smiliness in the streets of Beijing so it becomes second nature for residents. Once the smiling volunteers start spreading their smiley cheer, other locals are supposed to catch the happy bug and soon everyone will forget that smiling for no particular reason isn't the way things have always been.

It's only a matter of time before an eminent sociology professor develops a Smilometer so they can graph the steady improvements in tooth display.

I get to the *boulangerie* and join a short queue while I pore over their wares behind a glass counter. It looks for all the world like a Parisian bakery. Except that nobody is French and it's much cheaper. But they have the surliness down pat. I'd like free samples of several breads rather than buy a pig in a poke but have no choice but to dive in and select the bread that looks most like a French stick.

As I'm about to be served, a buck-toothed teenager with a jagged fringe pops up from nowhere with a pre-packaged *pain au raisin* in hand. He has just picked it off the countertop display and catches the eye of the shop assistant. I try to shame him into retreating to the back of the line by treating him to a disappointed glare but he refuses to be embarrassed. He throws his money on the counter and legs it. Unless it's Voluntary Wait in Line Day, nobody seems to care much for queuing etiquette.

As the day has worn on, the smog has gotten worse rather than better. Any hope that this may have been early morning mist has evaporated. I'm keen to get home as quickly as possible but I'm not about to start running because that might necessitate taking deep breaths.

Having inhaled thick poisonous gases on the way to the bakery, I think it would be best if I stay holed up in my apartment and wait for the smog cloud to pass – or be blasted into a torrential downpour by the WMO. I've also decided to shelve plans to visit the Great Wall of China until visibility improves.

Officials acknowledge that visibility has been particularly bad in recent days but they prefer to attribute this to fog rather than smog. Their spin is that the weather, rather than pollution, is primarily to blame for the fact that the city is grinding to a halt. The airport came to a standstill for several hours today and motorways were closed because drivers couldn't see the car in front of them. But again, we can shrug our shoulders and blame it all on freakish fog.

Official Chinese television and radio don't like to highlight pollution so I turn to the internet for some perspective. An Indian website informs me that 400,000 people a year die in China as a result of pollution – I wish I'd read that before I booked my flights from Dublin. Not only that, I find out that the weathermen went on Chinese media early today to warn the young and old to stay indoors rather than risk pulmonary infection. Thanks for the heads up.

Sorting out the pollution really would ease culture shock and make the city easier to adapt to for foreigners. But the rush to embrace western manners has me wondering just how Chinese Beijing will be in ten years' time. It was a mix of laziness and naivety that allowed me to wish that globalisation had homogenised cultures to the extent that it's possible to live in any modern capital. We're not all the same and that's for the best. Travel wouldn't hold much appeal if it weren't for the culture shock.

I'm dying to tuck into this bread roll but the crusty lump I've pulled off the end is not encouraging. It appears to have been glazed. Undeterred, I hastily rush through the process of washing and slicing tomatoes, draining the brine off a tin of tuna and smothering bread with mayonnaise. I have overly optimistic notions of recreating the kind of tuna salad roll that used to be a lunchtime staple back home.

Quelle deception! This is like no French baguette I've ever come across. It's soft, sweet and packed with fruit and nuts. It's more akin to the barmbrack you get at Halloween – except it doesn't even include a ring.

I don't expect China to cast off its customs or swap fried rice for hamburgers. But if they're going to embrace the delights of European breads, is it too much to ask for them to get it right?

I've a good mind to open a proper bread shop. Even the worst *boulangeur* in Paris would be a hit here. They'd be queuing around the block – at least on the eleventh of every month.

10

Volatility in Foreign Markets

utumn is the best time to visit Beijing. The weather moderates to a comfortable twelve or thirteen degrees and the wettest months are behind us. The sky clears a little as humidity drops and there's a spell of genuine 'blue days' until coal burning season brings an extra layer of smog. The leaves are heavy and brown and the evenings are mild rather than muggy. It is bliss. If only it lasted longer than a fortnight.

Alas, autumn appears to have come to an abrupt halt some time yesterday evening because it is now just four degrees and I'm not terribly keen to get out of bed. It's not even November yet so the temperature has a long way to fall before it hits the annual lows of January and February.

It hasn't mattered much until now that I've got tiled floors or that the front of my apartment is made of glass. When it's warm, the kitchen-cum-dining-cum-living area is as hot as a green house and the tiles are refreshingly cooling. Suddenly I'm willing to kill for a carpet and a decent set of lined curtains.

There are radiators in each room, including the shower room, but they can't help me now. The heating in my apartment complex – and in most blocks across the city – is centrally controlled. This doesn't simply put me at the mercy of the building manager; it means I await the decree of a Beijing bureaucrat.

The government decides when the heating is turned on for the entire country. For Beijing and other northern cities officials tend to plump for some time around November 15, by which time I expect to have icicles hanging from what would otherwise have been a runny nose. Even when the heat comes on, the authorities try to keep the indoor temperature at around sixteen degrees, which is not exactly toasty.

I have visions of a huge lever located somewhere in the basement of a Tiananmen Square civic office. It controls central heating for a billion people and it takes ten men to switch it on.

'Okay boys, let there be heat!'

I consider staying in bed until November 15 but, as that's two and a half weeks away, I eventually accept that this presents too many practical difficulties. Very slowly, I stick one leg out from under the covers, followed by the other and, a few minutes later, I drag the rest of my body out too. I've always been the type who prefers to dip a toe in the pool rather than dive straight in. And I'd rather remove a plaster one millimetre at a time than to tear the thing off in one brief but agonising instant.

The ceramic tiles cause pain as I tip-toe gingerly to the shower cubicle contemplating the pros and cons of hibernation. I fail to come up with a single con, as I switch the shower on and wait for the first thirty seconds of ice-water to swirl down the drain.

The showerhead is a cheapo plastic nozzle better suited to a watering can. It spurts water in all directions, which is another thing that has never bothered me much before.

Today is different. It seems logical that cold days demand the hottest showers so I crank up the temperature to the maximum. Ten long seconds later the mirror is steamed up. The water's ready but I'm stock-still, daydreaming about how many different types of animal devised a big winter sleep as a survival strategy. I'm being squirted by a thin cold sprinkle so decide that jumping into the spray is preferable to standing in the cold dry air. Bears, bats, badgers, snakes, squirrels, groundhogs and even wasps are known to snooze the cold days away. Why did humans never think of that?

'What time are you settin' the alarm for?'

'Nine o'clock on St Patrick's Day.'

My scalp is scalded by boiling water as I make a frenzied attempt to turn the temperature down. But despite the blast of heat, I'm still frozen. I settle on a medium temperature and proceed with the fastest shower of my life.

Scalded and shivering, I wrap myself in a towel and go back into the bedroom where I log on to the internet to see how long this living hell could last. Ideally, hibernating until April is recommended. That's when it becomes liveable again, even though they shut off the central heating in the middle of March.

Well, you can't change the weather.

I packed my bags for Beijing on a glorious July day in Dublin. The newspapers said the temperature in Beijing was hitting thirty degrees so I crammed my case with summer clothes: shorts, t-shirts, shirts, shades and flip-flops. I wasn't really thinking too far ahead.

So this morning I'm off to my local covered market in search of anything that might make the Beijing winter more bearable. The market is a ten minute walk away, just past the narrow bustling alley which plays host to Johnny's Place and a community of locals squeezed by inflation. Fortunately, prices in the market are affordable, especially if you are a regular customer, a Mandarin speaker, and an expert haggler. Some or all of these terms do not apply to me.

The market comprises four football pitch-sized barns as well as several cramped shop units set into its outer perimeter walls. It has everything from clothes, household appliances and food, to services like key cutting and shoe mending. I walk around the outside first where bargain hunters can go nuts in the Two Yuan Store. There's a heavyset woman sitting outside roaring 'liang kuai, liang kuai' – meaning two yuan, which is the equivalent of 20 cent – at nobody in particular. Her vacant face tells me she is on autopilot and has probably been reciting the same two words since she was a child. Of course this was probably the One Yuan Store before inflation kicked in so at least that brought some variety to her work.

Tea-towels, corkscrews, bath mats, chopsticks, key rings, pencil-parers, milk jugs – all for two kuai.

I acquire a hard plastic bottle of a type that half the country uses to carry their daily dose of tea. Even on sweltering summer days, Beijingers can be found sipping tea from their personal flagon. They're like hip flasks for tea-aholics. The shopkeeper holds up four fingers as I hand over a ten kuai note. Due to my lack of linguistic confidence and, of course, ability, I'm not in a position to query her when she returns six kuai and reverts to robotically bellowing 'liang kuai' at passersby. Four kuai? In the Two Yuan Store? Seems like false advertising to me.

Either inflation has hit 100% or I'm the victim of Big Nose tax. I suppose my new flask would be well worth 40 cent in Ireland, but that's the kind of thinking that encourages traders to charge foreigners more than locals.

The shopkeeper is catatonic and I can't bring myself to snap her out of it just so I can treat her to my incomprehensible Mandarin. So I grumble and move on.

Two men are repairing punctures outside a key cutting shop while two women discuss whether a torn denim shirt can be mended. In the next unit, which is the size of a photo booth, a teenage girl is putting a new sole on shoes that look fit for the bin. That's where my mindset differs from theirs. Cheap consumer goods – mostly made in China – have become disposable in the West. If it breaks, we throw it out. If it doesn't fit, we give it away. If it goes out of fashion, it goes in the Oxfam bag. We have plenty to learn from the Chinese on this score.

I walk into the first covered section of the market through thick plastic drapes which were once transparent but are now grubbily opaque. They are selling blankets, towels, wool and thermal underwear – just the sorts of things you need when somebody else controls your central heating.

Prices seem to vary wildly depending on who's buying, so avoiding the top rate of Big Nose tax is the main aim. To do this, I'll have to wheel out a little *Putonghua,* which means common speech – in *Putonghua.*

I had expected to be well equipped to survive the market. Once you can communicate about prices, and learn the techniques of a hard-balling master haggler (see Chapter 4), you can't go far wrong. Or so I presumed.

Of course, the Chinese have found a way to make expressing numbers a little more complicated than I had first imagined. Not all the usual hand signals apply.

If you want to buy things in quantities of one, two, three, four or five, simply hold up the corresponding number of fingers. When you want a couple of beers, you flick a 'V' sign – no offence is taken. But six beers would be a different story. For that you'd need to make the kind of sign you might affect when saying 'call me': tuck in your three longest fingers and hold out your thumb and baby finger.

The hand signal for the number seven looks a bit like an Italian who wants to emphasise their point: touch the tips of all your fingers together and try to resist pulling a face like Marlon Brando in *The Godfather.*

For eight, use your thumb and forefinger to make an L-shape. It's what kids do when they haven't got a toy gun. Nine looks like you've made a hook using only your index finger. The other fingers are tucked in as though you're making a fist. Easy?

Just to keep us on our toes, there are two options for ten. One is waving your fist as though you're threatening violence; the other is to use your index fingers to make a cross. Marching into a fruit shop and holding up all ten fingers in the hope of ordering ten bananas will make you look like a lout so mind your manners.

If you think that's a little more trouble than necessary, let me share what little wisdom I have amassed about the Chinese language. As you'll recall from when I tried to ask that weird gummy elf where I can access the internet, Mandarin is a tonal language. This means that the meaning of words depends not just on their sounds, but on the pitch you use to pronounce them.

The first tone hits a constant high note; it doesn't rise or fall. The second rises as you pronounce the vowel sound at the end of a word. The third is a funny one. It falls first then rises quickly. All of this is done on a single syllable, by the way. The fourth tone starts high and falls to a much lower pitch.

The word 'ma' is the classic example for how tone can change meaning. Using tones one to four respectively, it means mother, hemp, horse and to scold or swear. It leaves plenty of scope for misunderstandings, and opens the way for scores of mother-in-law jokes. Oh and there's also a secret fifth pitch which is a flat 'toneless' tone. This is tagged on to the end of sentences to indicate that you're asking a question. Got it? The sentence 'Ma, ma, ma, ma', where each one is pronounced in a different tone, means did mother scold the horse?

The Chinese characters familiar to westerners – if only because they are the symbols on top of the take-away menu – are known as *Hanzi*. Characters generally correspond to one syllable but can be amalgamated to give additional meanings. In a move supposed to standardise *Hanzi* and make things a little easier, so-called 'simplified Chinese' was introduced in the 1950s. The previous system then became known as 'traditional Chinese'.

So there are now two sets of symbols. Some of the traditional Chinese characters are identical to the newer simplified versions, but others are unrecognisable to their previous form. I can't discriminate between the two as they are both equally impenetrable to me at present.

Several attempts have been made to represent the Chinese language using the Roman alphabet. These are meant as pronunciation tools, although the notion of replacing *Hanzi* altogether with the European alphabet has been floated in the past by Chairman Mao, amongst others. It seems unlikely that a system of writing that has survived over 3,500 years would ever be scrapped, even though that would be really handy for me.

The two most commonly used systems for writing Romanized Chinese are Wade-Giles and Pinyin. The former was developed in the nineteenth century by a British diplomat by the name of Sir Thomas Francis Wade and later refined by a Cambridge professor called Herbert Allen Giles. This is the system that approximated the sound of China's capital as Peking but it has since been firmly replaced by the Pinyin which gives us Beijing. Neither is perfect but the latter is closer to the current local pronunciation.

Pinyin, which literally means 'spell sound' in Chinese, was officially introduced by the Chinese government in 1958. The government only began enforcing Beijing as the official name in the 1980s which explains why Peking is still so familiar. As far as Chinese people are concerned, the name of their current capital has never actually changed. In fact most are not aware that westerners can be confused by the two spellings.

The Pinyin system is taught to primary school children and is commonly featured on street signs and, if you're lucky, menus. It is recognised by the UN and International Organization for Standardization, so it looks like Wade-Giles will be consigned to history's scrapheap. The two were quite similar but the handiest feature of Pinyin is that the tones are drawn in over the vowels so you know whether to use a rising, falling or flat pitch. Unfortunately, while the system uses letters which will be instantly familiar to English-speakers, the sounds they represent are not always the same as in English. 'C', for example, sounds like 'ts'. 'Q' is a bit more like 'ch'. Gas, isn't it?

There are some other little snags worth mentioning but I don't want you to be as wholly intimidated as I am so let's not dwell on the hard parts too long.

The Chinese use 'measure words' when discussing quantities. A number isn't enough. It's a bit like having to ask for two *bottles* of milk rather than just two milks. Nouns considered as belonging to the same category take the same measure word. However, things aren't grouped in a way that a western mind might relate to. They don't lump all types of furniture together or use the same word for all sports equipment. Things are categorised based on their size and shape. So, flat rectangular things – like tables, beds and maps – are given the same measure word. The same goes for things with handles like knives, umbrellas and toothbrushes.

Don't panic, it's not all bad. If you've tried to learn European languages you'll take some comfort from the fact that there are no masculine or feminine nouns. And the form of a verb is the same no matter whether you're using the first person ('I'), second ('you'), third ('he') and so on. Better still, you needn't worry about tenses because it's generally a matter of inserting an additional word to indicate you're talking about the past or future. The grammar is relatively straight forward as a result.

But before you head off to master Pinyin, the tones, and the traditional as well as simplified scripts, it's only fair to warn you that this isn't going to equip you to converse with all of China's 1.3 billion inhabitants.

Standard Mandarin is what Beijingers use and this predominates on national television and in print. However, the Shanghainese have their own lingo; Hong Kong and the southern provinces prefer Cantonese and there are scores of minority languages to be found across the country. Even some of the dialects of Mandarin are said to be as alike as English and French. *Merde.*

I wish I knew the word for 'wooly hat' – my ears are numb.

I meander through the market smiling politely at salespeople eager for me to inspect their wares. The closer you stand to the goods, the more likely you are to invite a sales pitch so it's best to keep your distance until you come across what you want. I happen upon two neighbouring stalls which stock a combined total of around 100 varieties of headwarmer. With minimal fuss, I pick the least ridiculous one and ask how much. 'Duo shou qian' literally means how much money.

That'll be 25 kuai I'm informed. I offer 15 but am dismissed by the angry vendor who goes off on a rant as though I've tried to steal her children's lunch money. It'll be 25 kuai and that's the end of it, says she. As I weigh up whether this is a good deal, a young mother arrives on the scene with babe in arms. She inspects a pink Hello Kitty hat that looks to my eye to be made of the same low quality polyester/cotton mix as the one I inquired about. My listening comprehension is woeful but I clearly hear the stall owner say it's 15 kuai. I watch in disbelief as the mother tables a bid of 5 kuai and they settle on 8.

I butt in to offer 8 for the hat I was interested in as they exchange cash and banter. No way, the seller says, before giving me a lecture which I think was about the high quality of the particular item I'm after. She'll give it to me for 20. If I hadn't seen the 8 kuai transaction I'd congratulate myself on my stellar haggling skills, but instead I wave her goodbye and visit the next stall.

I've never owned long johns and never expected to. However, the temperature can plummet to −17 degrees Celsius in January so I open the bidding at 20 kuai on a giant blue baby grow. Like all openers, this is laughed off and we eventually settle on 40. I bag my purchase and skedaddle before a regular customer arrives and buys one for 15.

Feeling a little more confident, I also snap up a hat for 12 kuai and a pair of gloves for 10 and take myself to the next barnful of merchandise.

The market's second section is selling jeans, suits and shoes of a style that hasn't quite been outdated long enough to qualify as retro. There's no way I'm haggling over a pair of two-tone baggy cords so I move on to the third section where they're flogging homeware. Here I purchase a small mat that will take the sting out of the early morning tiles, and a couple of coffee mugs for warming cold hands in winter.

The ferocious stench of piss that lingers in the ten foot space between barns three and four almost burns the back of my throat with its acidic vapour. This lane clearly serves as a public toilet but there's also a running tap where you can refill your flask.

I hold my breath until I'm safely inside the final section, which turns out to be the food market. I inhale a deep lungful of assorted smells. It's a mix of raw fish, meat and spices which brings on a minor head rush.

My toes are suddenly cold. The floor in the food market is a giant puddle caused by melting ice which helps keep fish fresh. Damp, soggy feet are no fun when it's freezing and you've no heating.

I wish I'd worn plastic bags on my feet like we did when we were playing winter matches in the Under-9 football league. When it was really bitter, our goalkeeper would sport a black sack under his jersey so he didn't catch pneumonia waiting for action to come his way. It's not that we had a particularly mean defence, it's just that the pitch was so big that it took five minutes for our little legs to move the ball from one end to the other.

Blood-spattered people behind blood-spattered counters hack away at huge hunks of animal carcases in an attempt to harvest every last ounce of meat. It looks like a scene from the Texas Chainsaw Massacre. Vegetarians should steer well clear. So should cows.

Not for me the pig's head or live eels; I complete a swift lap of the hall just to feel like I've seen everything and bid the market farewell. The produce is a little too fresh in the food hall for my liking but overall I'm beginning to feel like a local Chinese punter at his local market. Or at least I would if they'd let me. Slapping a *de facto* Foreigner Tax on everything doesn't do much to make you feel like we're all in the same boat.

What little heat was on offer from the afternoon sun dissipates as it gets dark around 6.00 pm. The clocks neither spring forward nor fall back in Beijing so it's easy to see the days getting shorter by a few minutes every evening.

With scores of winter evenings stretched out in front of me, I reckon it's high time to give Chinese television a fair chance. I haven't felt the need for TV until now but quiet nights in are what John Logie Baird had in mind when he dreamt up the idiot box.

Here I sit watching television, drinking tea from my new flask, wearing extra-large long johns and my new hat. I'm boringly excited about battening down the hatches until spring and seeing what my old friend television has in store.

Things could be worse.

11

Good News from China

oap opera, Beijing opera, war stories, love stories, business news, more soap operas, volleyball, army bands, a talent show, and a kitchen-based cookery competition possibly entitled *Ready, Steady, Wok*. And it's all in Chinese.

I've done three full rounds of the forty-two channels on offer and the situation's not looking too promising. The least worst option so far is a talent show featuring singing kids smiling manically while dancing a lifeless dance around a drab stage. I bet those kids are beaten. Anybody who expresses such happiness is surely desperately miserable.

The proportion of programming that involves military uniforms is arresting. Uniformed female singers entertaining the troops; troops entertaining bored-looking children; soaps set on army bases. Even one of the food shows feels like boot camp.

There's a boorish man with a callous, inverted smile and jowls like a pit-bull terrier sitting at a mahogany office desk which is covered with sliced fruit. He's wearing a uniform, of course, and intensely wagging his finger while delivering the sternest talking to I've ever endured. Of course I've no idea what he's saying but I feel like apologising and promising it won't happen again just so he might stop.

It's not clear what the fruit is about because he never looks at it, points to it or eats it. I'm spellbound. I should switch channels

A young security officer guards the
university compound

A restaurant preparing food
on the footpath

Red lanterns symbolise a warm welcome for foreigners

The 'Immortals' of Penglai

A Buddhist altar

Monks in Qingdao

Local statue of Mao

*A large Coca-Cola bottle
in a sculpture park*

Forbidden City rooftops

School run

Cable car at Penglai

The Great Wall

Three security guards in winter uniforms posing with the author

Bride and groom in Ditan Park

Men playing Chinese chess

Consumerism grips Wangfujing Street

Tiananmen Square

Cheap eats on a side street

An early morning workout at an outdoor gym

China under construction

*Monks leading a Buddhist
conversion ceremony*

but need to wait and see what happens next. Anyway I'd probably be in even more trouble with this sergeant major if I tune out of his lecture.

He thumps the table once, twice and a third time, before standing up abruptly as the credits roll at high speed. The fruit stays on the table as he walks out of shot and I begin to wonder what possible entertainment value or public service this bizarre show might have. It's going to be a long, dull winter.

I begin my fourth lap of the channels longing for a dose of RTÉ or BBC. Would Sky Sports be out of the question? Suddenly I realise I've skipped past what sounded like English. Flicking back two stations I find my new favourite channel – CCTV9. It must have been taking a commercial break while I whizzed through the stations moments earlier. I'm prone to trigger-happiness with the remote control.

In the English-speaking world, the acronym 'CCTV' is synonymous with security monitoring systems. Here, it stands for China Central Television. It's the state broadcaster with a bevy of sixteen channels, including China's only English language station, CCTV9. The network toes the Party line when it comes to handling politically sensitive stories which often makes for wacky but perversely intriguing viewing. It's high definition propaganda for the multichannel age.

I wonder whether the choice of naming the national broadcaster after surveillance equipment was done with tongue in cheek or was it just very unfortunate. Hopefully, the television set in my state-owned apartment block isn't like the two-way telescreens in Orwell's *1984*. I'll stop idly scratching my itchy bits while lounging on the sofa just in case I'm being monitored.

CCTV9 must become my channel of choice strictly by default: there is no choice. But even if I had access to all the Irish, British or American channels under the sun, it would be hard to tear myself away from this most fascinating and hilarious of news stations. Although, if there was a Champions League match on RTÉ2, that would probably win out.

I'm a hopeless news junkie and need to consume a daily quota of 100 useless facts or sleep will be impossible. I'm in training to be a pub quiz shark when I retire in a few decades. At present, it's difficult to win quizzes against people who can incorporate personal stories into answering questions like: 'What date were monitory systems decimalised in Ireland and the UK?'

'Oh I know this one and I'll tell you why ... It was the Monday after the Sunday which was Valentines Day of 1971. And the reason I recall Valentines Day was because I was off work with a broken leg since the Friday and couldn't go to a dinner dance with the bit of skirt I was courtin' on account of me injury ... I was wearing a dark green jumper that day; the same colour as the tie George Colley was wearing on the news the night before – although we only had a black and white telly back then so I can't be sure about that ... I forget who's round it is – is it yours?'

It's easy to answer history questions if you were there at the time.

The stories on CCTV tick few of the boxes required by news editors in the western media but it surely keeps the Party happy. Newsworthiness as I know it has been redefined. It's all about the government's good deeds; the expansion of Chinese companies; and why the US and WTO are unfair to little old China.

Tonight's lead story is a case in point: 'Chinese Premier, Wen Jiabao, visits old people for comfortable chat'. I enjoy a comfortable chat as much as anybody but it's not what I expect at the top of the evening news. Unless the story is that Elvis has popped into Starbucks for a chi latte, the consumption of hot drinks by old people should struggle to make it into the local newsletter.

It turns out that the spritely nonagenarians being treated to tea and sycophancy with Premier Wen were top scientists. We're told they are almost 100 years old but they could easily pass for eighty-odd. All three are an advertisement for spending your life in a lab brimming with radioactive material. In their day, they were involved in developing bombs capable of melting Japan, and their contribution to 'peace' is being recognised with a cup of tea.

It's riveting stuff. There are some stories that just can't be told on radio or in newspapers. You really need to *see* the tea to understand the story. What a scoop.

In truth, it is five minutes of the most banal television I've ever seen passed off as news. Perhaps the propaganda rationale behind running this non-story is that China wants to remind their neighbours that they've got big scary weapons. Or it could be that they want to make it look like the Premier is an affable chap who enjoys 'comfortable' – not stilted, mind – chats with old people. Then again, maybe they just want to increase tea consumption. I can't tell and couldn't care.

The second item on the news list comes from an international scientific symposium on pollution. Now that's a genuinely important issue that affects the daily lives of Beijingers so it's good to see CCTV hasn't ducked out of covering the event. The conference hall is swarming with experts and the roving reporter has managed to grab a quick word with three of them. But I can't help but feel there has been some heavy-handed editing. A snippet from one of the talking heads begins with: 'Despite this, there's reason for optimism and hopefully China can improve the situation.' Despite what?!

Next up is a special feature on the building of an enormous railway line through the finely balanced Tibetan landscape. Tibet is a sore topic with the Beijing government so there's always a sense that they are attempting to pre-empt criticism of their every intervention in the vast western region. They lose the rag when foreign governments say nice things about the Dalai Lama and Tibetan monks whom China brand as separatist enemies of the state. And they despise the interference of Richard Gere, REM,

Radiohead and other celebrity evildoers who highlight human rights and environmental atrocities in China's Tibet.

This must be why the presenter of the segment on Tibet's new cross-country railway line repeats the phrase 'the construction project caused no harm to the environment whatsoever' four times in ten minutes. That's no harm *whatsoever*. None. Get it? They doth protest too much.

You learn to decode propaganda after a while. It's like listening to political spin at home. If an Irish politician says last year's increase in health spending was even bigger than this year's increase, you know they are preparing the way for hospital cutbacks. In China, when CCTV reporters mention that some conference delegates to an environmental meeting said all was well but refers fleetingly to concerns over air quality, that really means the conference was dominated by a major row over Beijing's smog cloud.

By a distance, my favourite show on CCTV is the inaccurately titled *Dialogue*. The show usually takes the form of a two-person panel interviewed by a host on a pressing political or social issue. You might expect that the two guests would have different views, or that the presenter would press them for straight answers to tough questions. And you might be wrong. The show knocks a political ball around a confined court for thirty minutes, determined to reach no firm conclusion by finding increasingly inventive ways of expressing the official Party line. It takes considerable skill.

Take, for example, the issue of Taiwanese independence. It was to Taiwan that nationalist leaders fled in 1949 after defeat in the Civil War and the island has followed an altogether different path to its communist motherland. Taiwan retains the name Republic of China, it has its own currency, a separate government, it holds elections and has a flag. It's a more westernised country and has enjoyed considerable economic success.

However, the Chinese Communist Party in Beijing considers Taiwan to be a part of the People's Republic of China and they make sure the rest of the world sees it that way too. As part of its 'One China' policy, Beijing leaves no doubt that any country wishing to have diplomatic relations with China must ignore Taiwan's claim to be a sovereign nation. This doesn't stop officials from the island pushing foreign governments to recognise it as an independent state.

Taiwan's willingness to chance its arm in diplomatic circles extends to the highest level. The island regularly applies for some form of United Nations recognition, including sovereign status and full membership of the UN. China, which has a permanent seat on the UN Security Council, always makes sure the application meets with a resounding 'no way, Taipei'.

So it's a controversial and complex question which would be well worth a public debate on CCTV9. But instead we get *Dialogue*. Every question is essentially a paraphrase of: 'Just how wrong is Taiwan to seek UN recognition?' The responses range all the way from 'totally wrong' to 'very wrong indeed'.

The show specialises in soft, leading questions which invite pro-government answers. During a soporific debate on a speech by President Hu Jintao, guest contributors are quizzed on a range of key issues: 'China is in safe hands under the new Standing Committee, is it not?'; 'How bright is the future for the people of China?'; 'What feature of President Hu's speech most touched your heart?' What a grilling.

Under any media regime it can be tricky to decide whether news is objective. I'm not an expert on Taiwan, world trade or Asian politics so I turn to a field where I might claim some objectivity: international football. CCTV9's coverage of a friendly match between China and Japan is a case study in media bias. In a three-minute highlights package, the state broadcaster effectively claims that China was the winner of a drab scoreless draw. China's 'excellent goal chances' included an over-hit cross that dribbled harmlessly out of play and a back pass that forced the Japanese goalkeeper to casually adjust his footing before clearing the danger. What appeared to be Japan's only chance saw the old enemy carve the Chinese defence open before smacking a shot against the foot of the post and narrowly failing to convert the rebound.

Meanwhile, over on CCTV5 – the sports network – they are broadcasting extended highlights of the same game with Chinese commentary. No doubt the commentators are leaning towards their own heroic team, but the pictures didn't lie. Japan dominate possession and have the lion's share of the goal chances. In the end, China did well to come away with an honourable draw. It certainly wasn't the moral victory suggested by the news channel.

I don't care whether China is any good at soccer – I'd probably cheer them on unless they were playing Ireland – but if the state broadcaster is willing to apply heavy gloss to a football match, it's fair to presume the spin machine cranks up into overdrive when it comes to covering politics.

You'll be relieved to hear that CCTV regularly claims it will be making greater efforts at objectivity in future and its parent company has even provided it with consultancy services from international media experts, News Corporation. Rupert Murdoch's News Corp has some big names in its broadcasting portfolio including Sky and Fox News. We can expect CCTV to be 'fair and balanced' any day now.

The English language *China Daily* does for print what CCTV does for television. It's marginally less rose-tinted in that it acknowledges that various problems exist. However, it gives the impression that the government almost always has the answer to the world's woes. Its front page splashes, such as 'Party ready for Congress, says President', are every bit as outrageous as you might imagine, and the editorial page is home to uniformly hard-line communist perspectives. There's nothing wrong or shocking about communist views being expressed in a communist country, but the level of serious dissent is approximately nil.

Last weekend I got chatting to an English-speaking gent in The Rickshaw bar near Chaoyang's Sanlitun bar street. He works for *China Daily's* youth-focused sister paper *21st Century*. To protect his identity I'll withhold his name and country of origin. All I'll say is he hails from a country that borders Scotland and shares a name with the Prince of Wales. I jokingly shared my imagined vision of the *China Daily* office looking like a Soviet censor's headquarters. I see a small pool of dedicated journalists watched over by a row of Party hacks who scrutinise every word. 'That's pretty much how it is,' he said with an air of resignation.

With uniformly fawning coverage of Chinese politics available from TV and newspapers, I was sure that hope lay in the internet. Totalitarian regimes of the past never had to deal with such a vast open-access medium. Controlling the net just isn't feasible, I concluded. But I hadn't counted on the Great Firewall of China.

The government has invested over a billion dollars on a mammoth censorship project on which at least 30,000 people work to sanitise the web. They censor content, block sites and remove pages, as well as redirecting and filtering searches – aided and abetted by big-name multinational technology companies, I might add.

The Great Firewall of China is the nickname for Beijing's Golden Shield Project which began in 1998 as a reaction to the formation of the internet-savvy Chinese Democracy Party. Opposition websites are now inaccessible but so too is anything that could breed dissent among China's growing numbers of netizens. The authorities have blocked sites with political content, including tonnes of pages about Tibet, Taiwan and, of course, the 1989 Tiananmen Square incident.

Perhaps a little more bizarrely, all pages from BBC News were, until spring 2008, spiked, as was Wikipedia. I surely have my own inherent biases, but the BBC is hardly a subversive or reckless media organisation. It must have dirtied its bib with Beijing by publishing mean things about pollution or corruption because its news content was for years strictly off limits.

By definition, Wikipedia is open to input from thousands of faceless editors and contains pages on everything from China's human rights abuses to media censorship. Of course, by preventing Chinese people from contributing to Wikipedia, its content has become progressively more anti-Chinese making it even less attractive to Chinese censors.

The government is equally uneasy about anonymous blogs where free opinions flow without accountability. They advocate a system of blogging whereby contributors use their own name and provide authorities with their home addresses just in case they speak out of turn. This hasn't done much to make blogging a phenomenally popular way to waste time in Chinese workplaces.

I decide to test the Great Firewall out by trawling for politically sensitive information and lobbing loaded search terms into Google. I scour for stories about the pollution conference in Beijing and, as predicted, find that the meeting was overshadowed by a row over whether China is doing enough to improve air quality and clamp down on river pollution. That was a little too easy so I try something more controversial.

'Tiananmen Square' brings up a few headlines about the violence in 1989 – as well as a link to a Wikipedia page – but none of these sites are visible. The only web pages about Tiananmen Square are those that provide tourist information. 'Thousands of people come to the Square every day. It is the must place to visit in Beijing City.' Indeed it is.

Just for kicks, I Google 'Great Firewall of China' only to find that each of the first ten results are blocked. I suppose any censor worth his salt will start by censoring information about censorship. Clickable links to the sites are displayed but the links are a dead end. Google has copped a lot of flak for cooperating with the filtering of its search results. This was a condition set down by Beijing as part of the deal that allowed Google enter the Chinese market. Google reckons its compromise will ultimately help open China up to the wider world, but groups like Human Rights Watch and Amnesty International disagree. The websites of both of the latter organisations are blocked.

I had hoped to set up a blog while in China before they go entirely out of fashion. However, my Blogspot account, like a million others, is currently blacklisted. On any given day, the site could be completely down or fully accessible. More often than not it's possible to upload new blog posts but impossible to view your own pointless ramblings.

The government never issues statements or explains why it blocks or unblocks a site. Indeed, its censorship is fickle at the best of times. YouTube, for example, is usually accessible but from time to time will vanish temporarily. Shortly after I arrived, YouTube went down but Blogspot and Flickr returned on the same day. All three are owned by Google. The net was rife with conspiracy theories and rumour about why YouTube had fallen foul of the censor. Some said it was temporarily suspended for the duration of the Communist Party Congress; others reckoned China was punishing YouTube for launching a Taiwanese version of its site. Thankfully, normal service was resumed after a couple of boring weeks.

The expat bars in Chaoyang are abuzz with talk of proxy servers and techie tricks to circumvent the Great Firewall. You can, they tell me, access Blogspot via Japanese or US servers, thus conning the censor into thinking there's no direct connection between Chinese users and banned websites. Of course, these proxy sites are routinely added to the blacklist when they become too popular.

It's not much fun living with one of the most restricted media in the world. Surfing across the heavily sterilised Web, I happen across a reference to a report by Reporters Without Borders which places China seventh from bottom of its World Press Freedom Index. The Index is a who's who of repressive regimes. Unsurprisingly, my attempts to read the original document online are thwarted. With no hint of irony, the authorities have blocked the Reporters Without Borders website.

As I flit around the net looking for a detailed league table of the world's worst censors, my internet connection is abruptly severed. 'Connection to server was reset' is code for 'stop looking up stuff we don't like'. It will soon be among my most visited web pages. I suppose searching for everything from Taiwan to press freedom isn't a great idea when you live in Beijing.

Right before the connection was cut, I found a mention of Eritrea replacing North Korea at the bottom of the list. I bet nobody in either country has any idea what the World Press Freedom Index is. The same can be said for China.

Between working the local clothing market and getting over my fear of eating dodgy food in smelly laneways, I feel well on the road to settling in Beijing. However, the censorship is one of the toughest tests of my adaptability.

We all believe in some form of censorship when it comes to things that encourage abuse like child pornography and snuff movies, but the widespread stifling of political dissent is not something I want to get used to. I worked as a journalist and editor at home so the uniformity of opinion is a more enduring, niggling form of culture shock than the rampant spitting or air pollution.

Whatever about how it affects me, I'm wondering what impact it has on the one billion people who have never known any other system. Do you learn to be selective when expressing your honest beliefs, or do you just stop forming your own opinion because it's too much trouble?

I have decided to watch my entirely legal copy of *Babel* on several occasions but never seem to get around to it. Now though, with my internet connection down and CCTV9 showing a glorious reconstruction of Mao Zedong's military victories, it seems like the only available option. I put the DVD on and plonk myself onto the couch. Unfortunately I seem to have forgotten that my couch has as much give as a car roof and is not fit for plonking. I suddenly miss every couch I've ever sat on in Ireland and I blame censorship for this culture shock relapse. I could live with a hard couch if I had a couple of decent English-language TV stations and an internet connection that's not monitored by Big Brother.

After about an hour watching *Babel* I suspect the disc may be skipping. This isn't a side-of-the-street-five-kuai jobby. I purchased this product in a shop with uniformed staff, display shelves and its own roof. Surely official DVDs aren't as unreliable as the dodgy merchandise for sale outside my local supermarket?

The film plods along to a scene where a Japanese police officer finds himself alone in an upmarket apartment block with the daughter of a man he's investigating. She gives him the eye, he raises an eyebrow, and after a few deep and meaningless silences she appears set to disrobe. A brief blip later and everybody is almost dressed again but something significant must have happened because the cop is wrapping the barely-clothed young lady in his coat.

It soon becomes obvious that some kind of romantic fumbling took place but it has been cut out – censored, if you will. I'm presuming that was the best bit of the whole film. My personal opinion on the movie is that it was well-meaning twaddle. But that's just me – you can make up your own mind.

12

See You Later Innovator

'I'm Wendy and I teach English. If I had to describe myself I would say I am a very weak person. But maybe I am a good mother, despite my weakness of character. Thank you. Sorry.'

'Thanks to you, Wendy. Okay who's next? Jade, it's your turn.'

'Welcome to China. I am Jade. You are all handsome and beautiful and we are not. Thank you.'

'Very good. Wang Bo, could you introduce yourself and welcome our guests?'

'I am Wang Bo. I have no English name because that would be an insult to my Chinese parents. You are like movie stars and I want to learn your body language.'

Okey doke. It's introductions day at the university campus and the foreign teachers – of which there are thirteen – have been listening uncomfortably to the outrageously humble, often self-loathing presentations by the Chinese staff of the Foreign Languages Department.

It has been awkward. Where do you look when somebody you've never met is summing themselves up with words like 'weak' or 'useless'?

Once the excruciating self-flagellation is out of the way, the spotlight turns on the foreigners. There are seven Americans, three Canadians and three Irish.

I am not keen to go first. Our new Chinese colleagues are leaning forward expectantly waiting for somebody to speak. I'm not sure what kind of information is appropriate or whether I should follow the Chinese example by saying I'm an awful waste of space.

Luckily, this dilemma is taken out of my hands by the fact that I'm surrounded by eager Americans vying with one another to make the best first impression. They disregard the humility proffered by our hosts and launch straight into stunningly well-prepared self-promotional speeches. There's nobody like the Yanks for the hard sell. I feel like reminding them that this isn't an interview – they've already got the job – in the hope that they might tone it down. But I'm too busy taking mental notes and wondering how on earth I'm going to follow their lead.

Some of my new colleagues bound around the stage like attention-hungry nine-year-olds; others adopt a more professorial demeanour. We've all landed these jobs because we speak English and went to college in a developed nation. Those are the only prerequisites. That doesn't stop my colleagues – all of whom are older than I am – from listing their every scholastic achievement and talking about why they were drawn to 'academia' in China. Seriously folks, we just teach. Nobody is doing academic studies or leading research teams. An honest introduction would be: 'I was jammy enough to have been brought up in an English-speaking country so I'm working here because it's an easy way to get a respectable job and a visa while doing a bit of travelling. Cheers.' But I'm not about to introduce that degree of honesty into the mix.

Still, my verbalised CV feels a little thin, partly because the others are so damn good at selling themselves and because they have been alive longer than I have. All I can do is talk about the jobs I had before I got here and why I chose China's capital instead of Paris, Tokyo or Timbuktu. This is the question I've been struggling with since long before I packed my bags. But all eyes are on me so there'll be no ducking the issue this time.

'Beijing was an obvious choice for me. Right now, it's the most exciting city in the world's most interesting country. Everybody is talking about China because this is a time of great change, and to be here during the Olympics is something special. I want to be part of history.'

Whoa. Where did that come from? Did I say that? It's incredible what comes out when the collective gaze of fifty people is glued to you in anticipation. If necessity is the mother of invention, pressure is the father of bullshit.

It was slightly inaccurate to have said there are three Canadians in the faculty. One of my new workmates defies pigeonholing.

A severely earnest, pale and hairless man in his forties takes the floor once I've wrapped up my short spiel. I had lowered the bar to somewhere in between the American hyperbole and the Chinese rigmarole by resorting to talking about my passion for football after I ran out of things to say about my imaginary 'academic interests'. So the quietly spoken gent with an American accent and a morose smile has plenty of scope if he was looking for cues on how to pitch his introduction. A thin lanky strip of serenity, he begins thus:

'It might help you to think of me as a Canadian. That would be easy ... but actually I'm a person of the earth.'

He's also a committed communist, a software developer and the CEO of a start-up (one-man) IT company. Add to that the fact that he is applying to become a Chinese citizen and he's quite a ticket. He's also the best prepared schmoozer I've ever come across.

Business cards are a big deal in China. Everybody has one. They hold them between their thumbs and forefingers and present them two-handed to new contacts. It's best to receive them using both hands if you want to be polite. The Chinese put great stock in *guanxi* which translates as your sway with personal contacts or degree of social influence. It's a lot like the unspoken system of 'I'll scratch your back if you'll scratch mine' that operates in the West, but people in China are more open about calling in favours. In any case, it's easier to get things done here if you know somebody who knows somebody. *Guanxi* oils China's wheels.

Some of the western teachers have already had cards made but the formerly Canadian, future Chinese, earth person beats them all. He has devised what's called a Personal Networking Document. It's a four page description of his various business, academic and social interests which aims, we're told, to maximise efficiency in identifying areas of common interest with a view to social synthesis. That's a lot of bullshit for one who's under no obvious pressure.

Despite the intensity of listening to so many new teachers spouting on about themselves for three hours, it is announced with great gusto that the Foreign Languages Department is taking the newcomers out to dinner so we can endure one another's company a little longer. And so, like a line of ducks, we march half a mile down the road to an upmarket restaurant. One of the Americans is almost killed while narrating a home video about how dangerous it is to cross the street in Beijing, but remains hopelessly oblivious to the sound of beeping horns and screeching breaks. I don't want to see anybody being hit by a pedicab, but it would have been the perfect illustration for her video blog. And maybe just a small bit funny.

The restaurant is a culinary treat. We sit around a huge table in a private room reserved by the university. Tray after tray of food is brought to the centre of the table which rotates to help you try a little of everything. The slow-roasted spicy beef melts in the mouth; the crunchy garlic broccoli makes me wonder why I've never made it myself; and the fried pastry with soft apricot paste in the centre is surprisingly sweet but somehow savoury all at once. It doesn't matter much that the calamari is a little rubbery; that there's too much fat on the lamb or that the huge fish is bony and hard to pick up with chopsticks. Everybody just eats what they want and the servers keep the good stuff coming.

The head of the International Affairs Office, Mr Zhu, kicks things off with a lengthy and heartfelt welcoming speech. Chinese people are great hosts, he insists and, to prove it, he pops the cork on a porcelain bottle which we're told costs 300 yuan. This must be the good stuff. It's *bai jiu*, the spirit I'd overindulged in with Johnny in the downmarket laneway on the wrong side of the dual carriageway outside. Tonight's tipple is twice as strong and in the interest of giving us a good reception, Mr Zhu waits for all glasses to be full before issuing a hearty 'gan bei'. If you were paying attention you'd know that's the cue to drain your glass. And we do. Many, many times.

As proceedings wear on, Mr Zhu seems to be on his feet every five minutes making ever more heartfelt and emotional toasts – all of which end with 'gan bei'. As different dishes come our way, wine, beer and juice are poured to complement the food. Drinking is mandatory and sipping is prohibited. Glasses must be drained unless you've got something against the host, his family and the People's Republic of China. By the end, we're all fairly sloshed and our host's speeches have become so long-winded that nobody pays much attention when he rises with glass in hand to thank us for helping China become a great nation.

Dinner had begun around 6.00 pm so by the end of the evening – 9.30 pm – we are all the best of friends and I've forgotten how irritating they all seemed in their introductions. My American colleagues, like all decent US citizens you meet outside the security of their homeland, have been at pains to stress their Democratic credentials and accept that the Iraq war wasn't a great idea. *Gan bei* to that.

As we get up to leave, one of the Chinese staff from the International Affairs Office invites me to do a PhD at the university, and between the flattery and the *bai jiu* I seem to be agreeing in principle that this would be a superb idea. It will require six months of classes followed by a research thesis which can be written in English. They'll pay the fees and provide accommodation.

'Sounds great! But what subject would I be studying for this doctorate?'

'Oh that doesn't matter. Will you do it?'

'Sure.'

There's no way in hell that I'm doing it. By the time we meander home, the only thing I can conclude about the seemingly random invitation to take on a PhD is that the university is desperately keen to swell its ranks of overseas students. They couldn't care less what discipline the Big Noses study or whether they would be capable of staying the course. I'm also wondering how valuable a doctorate from a Chinese university could possibly be if students are accepted to research programmes over a feed of beef and beer.

Anyway, the accommodation on offer is a cell at the International Students dorm where I laid my weary head on a rock-hard prison bed for my first few nights in Beijing. That's the deal breaker.

With the introductions and hospitality out of the way, it's finally time to start work. Unlike the other self-styled academic Big Noses in the faculty, I have approximately zero experience teaching English. So, giving my first class in Advanced Writing is a little daunting. It sounds like a course I'd prefer to take than deliver.

I'm naturally worried about whether I'll be any use at teaching, but am equally concerned about classroom management and discipline. Having to spend time on crowd control and handling unruly students is the toughest part of teaching. I read that in a book.

The students here are postgraduates taking masters and doctoral degrees in science and engineering subjects. They are in their early to mid-twenties and billed as the best and the brightest China has to offer. These geeks are hand-picked from right across the country and are notoriously diligent, although one experienced teacher hints that standards may be falling because more and more students are being taken in each year.

I don't know exactly what to expect from the students as I make my way to my first class, but am surprised to find large love hearts cut out of pink card on the doors of all the classrooms. Written in English and Chinese is a message to teachers:

'Dear teacher, thank you for helping us achieve everythings we dreamt everyday with you're knowledge.' (sic)

Naturally, I correct the grammar in red pen and advise them to quit dreaming and start learning.

Is this the work of the next generation of innovators?

China is a young country with a median age of thirty-three. It's coming into its productive prime and has been gobbling up manufacturing jobs from western countries for a decade. They are experts at figuring out what American and European companies do and finding ways to produce goods cheaper and quicker.

Now the Beijing bigwigs have a new target. High-tech, high-end jobs – the kind that governments in developed countries reckon are safe from the low-cost Asian production lines.

The Communist Party has begun putting major emphasis on innovation through the state media. The language coming out of the ruling politburo echoes the kind of rhetoric now common in the West. It's all about fostering a 'knowledge economy' breeding invention and creativity.

Having first made carbon copies of our manufacturing products, the Chinese are now trying to mimic our innovation policy. But is this really possible? Is innovation, by definition, something you can't simply duplicate on the cheap in Asia? I intend to pick the bulging brains of my students in a bid to find out.

Using students for your own research purposes without consent is probably against some kind of teachers' ethical code, so it's times like this I'm glad I'm not really a professional teacher.

The classroom reminds me of my primary school. It has tiled floors and the white walls are bare but for a clock and a huge blackboard. The blackboard is green. The only major difference is that there's an overhead projector which is hooked up to a laptop to facilitate PowerPoint presentations. Microsoft was still in its infancy when I was in mine.

The students, sitting two to a desk, look surprisingly alert for 8.00 am and fall silent when I walk in. 'Good morning,' I say quietly. The crowd of forty students roars back 'Good morning!' with gleeful enthusiasm. They are so excited to see me that there are students in the room who are not even registered for the class. Extra chairs have been sent for so the people standing at the back can take the weight off.

What's going on here? Early morning classes are usually the victims of low attendance. I was expecting some sleepy students to stay in bed after a late night of partying. But not here. It's lights out at 11.00 pm and drinking is frowned upon. Young people go to college just to study. I'm suffering a culture shock relapse.

Students routinely sit in on extra lectures – just as a young Mao Zedong did back in the day – purely in the hope of learning something. I was initially told there would be eleven students in this morning's class but almost four times as many are now gaping up at me.

I ask everyone to stand up and introduce themselves, which is to invite forty overexcited children to tell you what an honour it is to meet a foreigner, usually followed by an invitation to visit their hometown – which is invariably described as the best city in China.

Some have taken English names like Lily, Wendy, Peter and Bruce, while others seem to have selected random words that they like the sound of. I've got a Bluestone, a Pointer, a Welfare and, best of all, a girl called Anyway.

Anyway, many students have learned English for over ten years but have never met a native speaker until now. Their awe for westerners and respect for authority is overwhelming. Students turn up early, they hang on your every word and they do their homework. Where's the apathy, the cynicism, the sarcasm?

If I told them reading *Ulysses* backwards while hopping around campus on one foot would help their English writing, they'd do it without question.

It's all a bit unnerving. I find myself longing for signs of individuality or a bad attitude from some smartarse who thinks they're too cool for school. But even the people at the back are listening. Surely one of them would like to sneer at the teacher. Nobody here is even remotely too cool for school. Appointing a class clown may be the only way to shake things up.

The first exercise I have planned is cogged from a TEFL textbook. It's a straightforward brainstorming session followed by an essay. I ask students to help me compile a list of successful people on the board, to say what they think of the person in question, and then to write 100 of their own words on what success means to them.

'So, who wants to give me the name of a successful person? Anybody? No volunteers? Okay, Bluestone, name a successful person – anyone in the world.'

'Chairman Mao, because he is a great man and the father of modern China.'

I should have known. Nobody dares dissent from this view when I ask whether Mao had any failings, so I move swiftly on. The rest of their heroes are sports stars like NBA basketball idol Yao Ming and table tennis legend Deng Yaping. One scallywag shows a hint of spark when he suggests Bin Laden was technically successful in achieving his aim of attacking New York but nobody is tickled by this apart from me.

Their views on success and just about everything else tend to be painfully uniform and politically correct for a supposedly diverse bunch of postgraduate students from across the country. It's hard to tell whether they are offering genuine opinions or simply saying what they think they are supposed to say.

If it's the latter, this may be due to the constant threat of surveillance. I had been warned by an American colleague that an observer sat in on her first few classes last year. These school spies don't participate, they just stand at the back of the room passively keeping teachers on their toes. This, she surmised, was to make sure she wasn't spouting capitalist propaganda in a communist-run school. I'm treated to the same scrutiny, but I brought it upon myself.

I had ill-advisedly attempted to generate some debate by discussing an article on illegal organ trafficking. China is often criticised for failing to clamp down on the practice but I wasn't about to dish out a lecture in morality on my first day. However, I was hoping it would be an issue they would be familiar with and might have a range of views on.

For the last thirty seconds, a pair of beady eyes has been peering through a square of glass in the middle of the classroom door reading my slideshow about back-alley kidney harvesting.

In hindsight, I really don't know what possessed me to try stoking a debate in a university. Next time I'll just waffle on about the runaway success of China's economy. Everybody can contribute to that one-sided discussion.

Predictably enough, the observer walks in and makes his way to the back of the class. He's middle-aged, pudgy and wearing the top half of a cheap grey suit over ill-fitting black trousers. His large thick-lensed plastic glasses look like those sported by North Korean dictator Kim Jong-il.

Hesitating and stuttering, my teaching style goes to pieces as I attempt to choose my words as carefully as a panda picks a partner. The pressure breeds five minutes of bullshit about there being no right or wrong when it comes to selling organs to sick people as I skip through my slides on illegal organ trading. My original plan for a class debate on the subject is unceremoniously binned as I abruptly return to the safer ground of introducing myself.

I ask the class what they know about Ireland and am surprised by the range of responses. Robbie Keane is better known than Roy Keane; everybody knows Westlife but few know U2; most think Braveheart is about Ireland; and while some have no idea where Ireland is, the more worldly students either think it is part of Britain or that there it is a nation gripped by civil war.

I side-step the political stuff and concentrate on the important business of educating them about Roy Keane and advising that the hard-working lads in Westlife are not usually hero-worshipped by twenty-four-year-old male postgraduate students.

After class I am surrounded by a dozen students keen to drag out the lesson. The observer is amongst them, monitoring the conversation but saying nothing. I ask a group of sporty-looking fellas what music they like, apart from Westlife. Ask the same question of college students in the West and there'll be a competition to name the newest or most obscure Indie band that has yet to break into the mainstream. My students rave about US heart-throbs the Backstreet Boys, and British chart toppers Blue.

Now, prefabricated boy bands have had their place since the Monkees. And although I'd rather fill my ears with molten lava than listen to N'Sync, it has to be accepted that teenybopper girls are entitled to pester their parents into buying posters of whatever crop of effeminate male vocalists the record companies are pushing in any given month. But I worry about their popularity among the supposedly discerning audience of twenty-something male students.

The more I get to know my students, the more immature they seem. They have had their heads in text books since they were old enough to read and are under immense parental pressure to land a big job and provide for their families. Many students' parents have chosen their college courses and mapped out detailed career paths. To deviate from the prescribed route is to fail, and to fail is unthinkable. Families make great sacrifices to support college-going offspring and the unwritten agreement is that once these aging adolescents graduate, it is payback time.

There are a couple of major flaws in this social contract. Firstly, students have willingly devolved total control of their lives to their parents who make each and every decision for their adult children. This level of handholding is not conducive to independent thought, so I'm blaming the parents for producing a generation of boy band fans.

But the problem is even more serious than the shocking popularity of the Backstreet Boys. These postgrad students are supposed to be innovative thinkers. We keep reading that this generation of Chinese is lining up to take our 'high value' jobs and will be lording it over us all by 2020. I cannot and will not answer to a middle-aged Boyzone fan.

On top of kowtowing to their parents, university students are restricted by China's totalitarian approach to dissent. With observers safeguarding political correctness in the classroom and the mass media toeing the Party line, the prospect of producing free-thinkers is slim.

The government wants innovators and creative problem-solvers but still expects intellectuals to shut down the half of their brain that might otherwise criticise the political system. It seems counterintuitive to suggest that some of the brain's creative centres can be ossified without affecting others.

Originality is a rare quality in the student essays I correct, while plagiarism is commonplace. China can churn out all the low-grade PhDs it wants but if I were a western leader, I wouldn't panic about losing the innovation war with the east. Original thinking is the one thing that can't be pirated.

Millions are buying into the idea that third level education is the key to making China a great nation but this could have potentially disastrous consequences for Beijing. The Party has looked at how developed nations pour money into the university sector and done its usual copy and paste job by replicating this model on a mass scale. Conventional wisdom suggests education improves society. Knowledge is power, education is freedom and all that. The trouble is that the Chinese have been too successful.

There has been a five-fold increase in the number of university students in China since 1999. The Department of Education says this is a fantastic achievement given that it usually takes developing nations decades to produce so many graduates. However, the wily President Hu Jintao is using more measured language. He favours slowing the breakneck speed of China's success so it can be managed.

There are now 25 million people in Chinese universities. Around five million students graduate every year with degrees and high expectations. Sadly, there are too few suitable jobs. Up to 60 per cent of graduates cannot find employment. These are the young people on whom the hopes and financial futures of an extended family may be pinned. The competitive jobs market forces some to take low-paying jobs while others are told they are over-qualified.

Meanwhile, there are not enough skilled people working in the trades. The focus on the university sector has been at the expense of vocational training. That's why when the lift breaks in our apartment building, they send for the untrained maintenance man who stares hopelessly down the elevator shaft without the first clue about where to start. He's the same guy who can't fix the air-conditioning, the bad wiring, the blocked sinks or the crumbling plaster in the kitchen. I suspect he may have designed our shambolic apartment from start to finish.

China faces decades of square pegs in round holes unless it can either attract the kinds of jobs it has trained young people to do, or begin diverting its workforce into becoming electricians, plasterers, fitters and lift technicians.

The number of 'overqualified' university graduates has been accumulating for several years and will continue to swell over the next decade. This is a time bomb with the potential to blow China's development off track if it's not diffused.

The worst case scenario by 2020 is that rural villagers will feel entirely left out of the economic revolution which is benefiting big business; the urban poor will have been priced out of the market for food and property; and tens of millions of highly educated young people will have little to do but bemoan how they've been short-changed by society.

Flash back to the Tiananmen Square in 1989. Those anti-government protests escalated as unrest among two main groups grew. Workers were upset by inflation and disaffected young people joined political dissidents drawn from a relatively small pool of students and intellectuals.

If the Party can't innovate its way past this dormant social volcano it will erupt before you can say 'unstoppable Asian superpower'.

13

Hitting the Wall

et's get one thing clear: you cannot see the Great Wall of China from space. Next time the quiz master at a charity table quiz asks, 'What is the only manmade object visible from space?' object vociferously to being asked an impossible question. If you smell any hint of a fudge – 'Okay, everybody gets a point. Doesn't matter what you put. It's a controversy we're not going to settle tonight' – stage a sit down protest until you are awarded maximum points for that round and everybody else gets nothing.

It doesn't matter if the quiz is a good-natured family fundraiser for sick children. There's a principle at stake. Stick to your guns until the self-appointed quiz master apologises to all concerned – especially the children – for spreading this myth.

According to NASA astronauts, the Great Wall can't even be seen from 180 miles up because it is the same colour as the surrounding landscape. And it certainly cannot be seen from the moon, which is 237,000 miles away.

The urban legend claiming that the Wall is so great that it can be seen from space with the naked eye began years before it was possible to test its veracity. It's hard to know exactly when this particular Chinese whisper was first uttered, but published references can be found as early as 1932 in a cartoon from *Ripley's Believe it or Not!* A similar assertion appears in Richard

Halliburton's 1938 *Second Book of Marvels*. Halliburton claimed that astronomers believe the Great Wall to be the only manmade thing visible from the moon. But you can't trust Halliburton. It was 1961 before Russian cosmonaut Yuri Gagarin made it into space on behalf of mankind, and Neil Armstrong didn't take his giant leap until 1969.

So, while it was impossible to know what is visible from space in the 1930s, it was also impossible to prove what's invisible. By the time astronauts could set the record straight, the legend was already deeply rooted in the public mind.

I could claim there's a secret branch of Starbucks in an invisible underground ice cave on Pluto's moon, but it'll be quite a while before anybody pays Pluto a visit and proves me wrong. Better still, philosopher Bertrand Russell once suggested that there was a tiny china teapot revolving around the sun in an elliptical orbit which was too small to see with even our best telescopes. He didn't really believe it of course; he was just being a mischievous philosopher. You know what those metaphysical rascals can be like. Russell's point was that the burden of proof should lie with those who make far-fetched claims. Otherwise, anybody would be free to state all sorts of nonsensical mumbo jumbo as though it were fact. As it happens, Russell was suggesting that the existence of God ought to be subject to the same rules as the existence of his teapot.

Apart from seeming intuitively ridiculous, the main reason Russell's teapot story or my Pluto claim won't become an unquestioned fact, while the Great Wall myth persists, is that we really want to believe that the Wall is visible from space. It suits us to think that man has constructed something so immense that it can be seen from beyond our own planet. 'We may seem insignificant on a celestial scale but damn it, we are making a difference.' Not to worry, you can probably see the smog from space so rest assured that mankind is making its mark.

It's 6.20 am on a fresh blue November morning and gusts of crisp air provide the smack in the face we need to jolt us into action. Why are there so many people up at this unholy hour of a Saturday? Scores of people are taking brisk walks to nowhere in particular while others bat ping pong balls back and forth. I hope they're not all warming up for a trip to the Great Wall. I was hoping we'd have the place to ourselves.

Girlfriend and I have packed a bag full of mandarins, cashew nuts, biscuits, water and a lunchbox full of pasta. After weeks of procrastination, we are finally set to visit the wall. This is the fourth week running that we've made a preliminary plan to trek across China's best-known wonder of the world. Every week there's an excuse: a party, a concert, a top-of-the-table Premier League clash. This time there's no backing out – not least because there's a 'small, fat woman with a little, blue car' waiting for us at Xi Da Qiao.

A colleague made an identical trip last week and has put us in touch with a Chinese driver who will bring us to a less-travelled section of the Wall. We're the type of sightseers who fancy ourselves as being a little cuter than the average tourist, despite actually relying more on chance than research or hard-earned travel nous. The busiest and closest section of the Great Wall is at Badaling. It's thronged with people, especially in the summer months, and is an excellent place to visit if you want to buy overpriced junk and be pestered by hawkers. Badaling's bit of wall has also suffered most from China's tendency to reconstruct its heritage with new materials and pass it off as an ancient ruin. We'll leave that to the plebs.

Our route will take us on the ten kilometre trek along the wall from Jin Shan Ling to Simatai. This is fast becoming as popular as Badaling but its distance from the city centre and treacherous terrain keep away the old, the young, the weak and the lazy.

We take the subway to Dongzhimen station near Chaoyang and hop on the 980 bus to Xi Da Qiao where our driver awaits. The bus station is teeming with dodgy characters vying to sell you junk or convince you to take a private bus for an extortionate price. We bat them all away and are lucky to find seats on the oversubscribed 980 express.

The bus takes a little over an hour, which means we are subjected to the ear-splitting sound of a bleeping handheld video game being played by the teenager slouched in the seat behind us for seventy minutes. Most people are trying to sneak a few minutes' sleep as we journey through the uninspiring landscape into which the dual carriage way cuts its course. Even though we couldn't possibly be the only passengers irritated by the selfish teen's electronic noise pollution, nobody bothers to tell him to pack it in. After half an hour of beeping, bleeping and buzzing, Girlfriend uses a combination of gesture, head-shaking and frowning to communicate her displeasure to the offending gamer. I supplement this with a tilt of the head that says, 'you better do what she says, sonny – you wouldn't like her when she's angry'. He duly packs it in.

The bus is staffed by a driver and a ticket-selling uniformed hostess. She's officious but friendly, and kindly remembers to alert us when our stop is approaching. As we descend the steps, half a dozen jostling men surround us. The bus has delivered us into the arms of a baying mob. They are shouting numbers and waving maniacally in a fierce competition for our attention. I would have expected this to be a bidding war between taxi drivers trying to undercut one another in a saturated market, but the figures being quoted are all the same. It'll be 250 kuai to be driven from here to the Wall. Presumably a master haggler could whittle this down to at least 200 kuai but nobody seems to be lowering their bid. Bloody cartels. Is there no Chinese Competition Authority?

Luckily, we don't need to trouble ourselves with negotiating a price, and gratefully push past the rabble.

In accordance with the scribbled note I'm carrying in my inside pocket, a small, fat woman is leaning out the window of a tiny blue car. She's wearing a thick claret cardigan and gypsy earrings, and she greets us with a cheery laugh as we hop in and slam the doors. Luckily, our driver already knows we don't speak Chinese so she just smiles, winks and puts the boot down. I don't trust winkers.

I'd read a few online horror stories about unlicensed tour guides taking the old B-roads through rundown villages in a bid to avoid tolls and police checks. And that's exactly the route our little blue tin can is taking. Apparently it's safest to take an official tour bus and stick to the straight, smooth expressway. But that'd be no fun.

We're careering down and up a hilly road covered in taupe sand and littered with six-foot bails of corn sheaths. The car rattles as we overtake a battered tractor on a bend and nip back onto our own side of the road just in time to avoid the trajectory of an oncoming motorcyclist. The old road meanders through sleepy villages where small pockets of the farming community live in dusty, rundown houses. It's a scene that probably hasn't changed for half a century. Apart from the incongruous sight of futuristic solar-powered streetlights, this is a lifestyle untouched by progress. The people look poor in a way that isn't found in central Beijing – even in the ageing hutongs.

One after another, tiny villages come into view before vanishing out of sight seconds later as we thunder through at seventy miles an hour. The roads have fallen into disrepair since the motorway opened and our compact four-wheeled capsule does little to cushion us from the potholes, lumps and bumps.

We survive a fascinating, if bruising, ninety minute journey and reach Jin Shan Ling intact. Our driver hops out earnestly and helps us buy our tickets, which cost 50 kuai each. We pay her 80 kuai to cover the taxi ride and she leads us to the starting point of our trek, before indicating that she'll pick us up at Simatai in four hours. She waves us off and we turn to face the wondrous wall.

Full of vim, vigour, zest and gusto, we decide it's a good time to have a break. Hastily dashing into action on a physically demanding ten kilometre course is how you do yourself an injury. So we walk up fifty-odd steps until we're standing on the wall and then we break out the pasta.

A sociable old woman with skin as saggy and wrinkly as an elephant seems intent on engaging us in chitchat while we wolf down what the Chinese call Italian noodles.

'What country?'

'*Ai er lan.* Ireland.'

'Oh very beautiful, very beautiful!'

'Have you been to Ireland?'

'No ... I am Mongolian.'

For some reason, when you tell people in China where you come from, they invariably say it's beautiful. It matters not whether your answer is Iran or Denmark, it's good manners to respond positively even if you've no clue whether the country in question even exists.

'Jehovahstan? Oh I hear it's lovely in the summer.'

A highly professional Chinese tour guide marches her twenty-strong army of Australian, British and American tourists up the steps beside us and begins a thorough overview of who built the wall and why they bothered. We chew our pasta shells a little slower to ensure we don't finish lunch before the guide finishes her spiel.

'Construction of the Great Wall of China began in the fifth century BC and it has been expanded, repaired and rebuilt throughout Chinese history,' begins the guide, with well-practiced enthusiasm. An Australian twang is detectable as she continues: 'The Wall was originally made of earth and stone and served as a fortress against northern invaders. Much of the modern wall was constructed by the Ming Dynasty which ruled China from 1368 until 1644. The Ming used bricks to rebuild the Wall as part of their strategy to keep the Mongols out of Beijing.'

With a chuckle that's hardly appropriate, the guide notes that up to three million people died building the 6,700 kilometre structure. One of the group blurts out, 'Well it was certainly worth it'. It was a reflex; they probably didn't mean it.

The guide goes on to confirm that the wall cannot be seen from space, despite the persistence of a myth stating otherwise. Half the tour group have sceptical looks on their faces while the other half nod knowingly. Smug bastards. I bet some of those nodders only learned that fact recently and are now acting like only an imbecile could ever think the legend were true. This doesn't apply to me, of course – I've known the truth for months.

'In keeping with its role as a fortress, the wall features hundreds of watchtowers and small barracks used for storing weapons and food. Soldiers could also send smoke signals from towers like this one,' she says, pointing to the roofless ruin twenty metres ahead. Plenty of the watchtowers are still standing but others have collapsed long ago.

'Large sections of the Wall – especially those nearest Beijing – have been rebuilt and repaired. However, sandstorms threaten to erode large sections of the Wall. A full survey of the Wall has never been conducted so it's not known precisely which sections are most likely to be lost ... Let's being our walk. It should take us less than four hours to get to Simatai. Please don't hesitate to ask if you have any questions.'

Thanks very much. Some of the tour group have been shooting disdainful looks our way while we've been lapping up the free history lesson. Is it unethical to earwig on a guided tour you haven't paid for? It doesn't dilute the experience for those who have paid. However, it does seem to annoy the whispering Welsh lady with her hands on her hips and fly goggles perched atop her curly head. She's grumbling to her bored-looking bearded husband who couldn't be bothered getting worked up about my earwigging, the Wall or anything else for that matter. If the Welsh woman had paid full attention instead of glowering at us she wouldn't have missed the bit where the guide confirmed that the Wall cannot be seen from space. It's people like her ...

The woman from Mongolia continues to catch our eye as we pack away our lunch and I naively take her up on her suggestion that she take our photograph. Having learned to freeze out the touts at Tiananmen Square, I can't believe I've opened the lines of communication at China's greatest tourist trap. Our new pal was sitting with several other women of a similar vintage when we arrived. They all wore yellow peaked caps and one by one, they befriended tourists and followed them along the path. As soon as we rise to our feet, our hanger-on does the same. She begins doling out advice uninvited. We try to shake her off by ignoring her and taking regular breaks in the hope that she gets fed up waiting for us. But she has played this game before.

We're gaining on a middle-aged American woman who is labouring up the first of very many sets of crumbling steps ahead. She is politely humouring a friendly yellow-capped tout who she seems to think is interested in finding out about what the weather is like in Tampa. As we overtake, the American is speaking very, very slowly indeed to the tout who is now holding her arm to assist with balance.

The unofficial guides in the yellow hats try to charge tourists at the halfway point for the invaluable help they have been along the treacherous trail. They also attempt to impose tolls on their supposed 'shortcuts'. If you're willing, they'll lead you along a grassy path which skips out sections of the Wall and shaves a few minutes of your time. Seriously, who comes to the Great Wall of China and then pays for a shortcut? It's like finding yourself 100 yards from the summit of Everest and asking whether there's a cable car to the top.

A particularly steep, dilapidated hill – which looks like it was once a flight of stairs – presents itself as we wind our way around one of the wall's many bends. It's the perfect opportunity to lose our ageing guide. As we roll up our sleeves and grapple with the forty-five degree stony slope, I feel a pang of guilt. For the sake of perhaps €5, we're fleeing from a sixty-year-old woman who would probably spend her Saturdays sauntering around a shopping centre had she been born in another country. Instead, she is reduced to pestering tourists for pocket money. It might ease my conscience if I go back and give her 20 kuai and a smile.

'You want to buy t-shirts?' she shouts as I mull over the merits of giving her a few quid. We pause and look over our shoulders at the kitsch rags she's waving above her head. '200 kuai,' she suggests. 200 kuai? Forget it. Greedy beggar. The guilt subsides in that instant and we clamber over the apex and disappear from her view.

I didn't expect the Wall to be as wavy as this. It snakes left and right, north and south, following the path suggested by the mountains. Would it be churlish to suggest it might have been an even greater wonder if they'd built it straight and smooth? I suppose it would then be overrun by yuppies on rollerblades.

We've been on the Wall for around two hours and no longer have need for the coats, scarves or gloves that were essential for survival at 6.20 am. Climbing up old steps and struggling to keep your footing on the way down gravelly slopes takes it out of you. The old tracker has long since given up on us, so we decide it's safe to take a break. We fix our sights on one of the many watchtowers up ahead, resolving to sit down for ten minutes once we've reached the landmark.

The watchtower is guarded by three men, one of whom is in uniform. All three have ID badges swinging from their necks. All three look shifty. It's 40 kuai to get through the gate, they say, as they flash their badges. Had I not been forewarned that this would happen I'd be fairly suspicious about this posse of likely lads who prefer not to make eye contact. But I hand over 80 kuai and ask how far it is to Simatai. 'One hour.'

We're way ahead of schedule. Too far ahead. Our driver is due to meet us in about two and a half hours so a lengthy break is in order. We tear open the bag of nuts, peel the mandarins and take the biscuits out so we don't forget them. The sun glows overhead; it's bright but distant. With the exception of the odd wheezing trekker, it's remarkably peaceful. The scenery – natural and manmade – is awesome.

We kiss and excitedly open the coconut bickies. They're a brand we've never tried before and curiosity is as good a sauce as hunger. Crunching on our biscuits with our backs to the Great Wall and our faces to the sun, we realise we're enjoying one of those moments that will stay with us for as long as our memories function. And, for a few moments at least, this provides a more than satisfactory answer to the 'What am I doing in China?' question. This is *it*.

We exchange a look, a smile that says, 'Are you thinking what I'm thinking?' The answer to that question is 'yes' and Girlfriend verbalises what's on both of our minds: 'These coconut yokes are all right but I'd give anything for a packet of Jacob's Polo.' So would I, my love, so would I.

Two English blokes are approaching. We can hear them before we can see them. I've decided that at least one of them must be a middle-aged Cambridge physics professor, purely by the sound of his booming voice. He is lecturing his companion on the virtues of Nikon digital cameras as though he were addressing an auditorium packed with 400 undergraduates seated on rows of staggered benches. It's all about lenses, pixels and memory capacity. As they come into view, the lecturer turns out to be about twenty-eight – a young fella – in a dandy full-length brown tweed overcoat. He's proudly wearing a weighty Nikon camera around his neck like it's an Olympic medal. His passive partner says little more than 'Yaw' whenever breathing demands that the lecturer pauses. The pair of them have side-partings that begin just above the ear, and they have invested in solid climbing boots and expensive wind-cheaters. They've got all the gear. As they pass at pace, Girlfriend and I agree they are products of the English public school system who breezed through an Oxbridge college and are taking a second gap year, having just completed their PhDs – one in economics, the other in organic chemistry. Their first gap year, when they were nineteen, was spent working with orphans in Kenya. It was ever so life changing. If all goes to plan, they'll get plum jobs in a Conservative government think tank.

A troop of German lads are next to pass our watchtower. The leader is a narrow, pale gent with a mop of orange hair. He looks Irish, apart from his round, thin, steel-frame glasses which are of a style perennially popular among northern Europeans. He's followed by a string of four of his compatriots who have all chosen a spiked blonde hairstyle that tells me they probably grew up east of that other great wall in Berlin. Struggling to bring up the rear is a wide-arsed, red-faced chap with spam-legs. He's wearing short shorts which he most likely hasn't worn in a decade. They are threatening to burst under the pressure. 'Hallo,' they say in turn as they pass. We offer a hearty 'Guten Tag' which amuses them greatly. They respond with something we can't comprehend so we offer a simple wave and they wave back with a chortle. A jolly bunch, the Germans.

Forty minutes later we are met by a rope bridge swinging in the wind between where we stand and the other side of a deep valley. A river flows rapidly beneath. It's the kind of bridge that belongs in an Indiana Jones movie. You can see him swinging from it after a baddy cuts the rope, or perhaps he could sprint desperately across as the latt's go up in flames one by one behind him. There's a sign which reads:

'Do not cross this bridge if you suffer from high blood pressure, heart complaints, infectious diseases, mental illness, alcoholism, confused state of mind or physical handicap.'

It's hard to imagine somebody who ticked any of those boxes making it this far but they must have some reason for the disclaimer. Perhaps a legless alcoholic had a heart attack on the bridge recently. The notice also states that there's a five kuai fee which will be collected on the other side of the bridge. Once again, I had been warned about having to shell out on three separate occasions and there's no alternate route – although Indiana would probably find a way – so we accept the toll and tip-toe across.

At the safe side of the crossing, we catch up with the German lads who are refusing to pay the extra levy. It's a point of principle rather than a matter of money. Like us, they paid 50 kuai at the beginning, 40 kuai at around the seven kilometre mark and now face another charge. But unlike us, they are willing to argue the toss for the sake of their principles. We undermine their efforts entirely by pushing past and paying up rather than standing shoulder to shoulder with our European cousins. I apologise as they step aside to let us through. 'Entschuldigung Danke shön. Danke.'

They reply in typically flawless English: 'But we are not German, we are from Holland.' I make the 'Oh right Ted' face and depart the scene to the sound of chuckling. A jolly bunch, the Dutch.

Within five minutes we've reached the end of the trail and turn to have one last look at the Wall, which has provided the highlight of our time in China to date. While you can't see the Wall from the moon, you could probably see the moon from the Wall, so cloudless is the sky overhead. That is more than can be said for most of Beijing's other sightseeing spots. Simatai is far enough from the city's smogosphere to have clear skies even when Tiananmen Square is blanketed in a cloud of soot.

As we take in the scene, it's tempting to hang about and test my claim that the moon is visible from a Great watchtower, but it's getting late and chilly so we're not sticking around.

There's another kilometre to walk downhill before we reach the pickup point where our little blue car and our small fat woman are waiting patiently. Just as we reach the foot of the hill, we hear a boisterous but distinctively posh roar: 'Geronimo!' The English fop whizzes by on a seat suspended from an overhead pulley system, his big brown overcoat flapping in the breeze. His quiet companion follows thirty seconds later clutching his mate's Nikon camera and looking terrified. The line runs from the top of the hill, above the river and delivers you to within spitting distance of the car park. It looks like fun – if you're Indiana Jones. We haven't the energy to climb back up steps to the take-off point so I don't even have to consider whether it's the sort of fun I might enjoy. Maybe next time.

Waiting for us as promised is our driver. She's playing cards with all the other drivers and isn't willing to leave until the game is over. She must be winning. When the driver's good and ready, Girlfriend and I slide into the back seat and the car whizzes off along the treacherous mountain terrain we survived earlier. It's probably for the best that we're too tired to care about our driver's erratic steering. She's beeping at oncoming traffic, swerving to avoid tiny children in tiny villages, and waving at friends when she should be watching the road. Her groceries are being thrown across the back seat, landing in our laps. But we couldn't care – just wake us up when we're near the station.

She kindly deposits us next to our bus and watches to make sure we get on safely. The sense of responsibility she feels for us is heart-warming, even if she did seem willing to risk our lives by overtaking a motorbike with a sidecar on a humpback bridge.

A couple of hours later, having dozed through the bus and subway journeys, we are dragging ourselves up the eight flights of stairs that stand between us and our bed. Of all the days for the elevator to be broken, this is amongst the worst. We feel flattened but wholly content. It is agreed that we'll round off the perfect day by watching a DVD in bed on the laptop, if our eyes will stay open long enough. I make the mistake of quickly checking my email when I should leave well enough alone. It's a horrible compulsion. Years from now, employers will face class action law suits from ex-employees who became email-dependent in the workplace and never managed to rid themselves of the addiction.

I have a message from Peter, a student who has been repeatedly asking me to play football with him and his classmates. He wants to play tomorrow morning at 8.00 am. A leisurely game of soccerball is something I'd been gung-ho about previously but having laboured on the Great Wall all day, I'd prefer a well-earned Sunday morning lie-in. Still, it's hard to turn down the offer when it's put in such typically flattering Chinese terms:

'Dear Gary, in reference to our past discussions regarding football. It would be our great honour and pleasure to have a man from the true Kingdom of Football join us in sport this Sunday morning. We will wait for you in room 301.'

The 'True Kingdom of Football'? I'm sure I told him I was from Ireland.

14

The Beautiful Game

I present to dorm 301 just after 8.00 am and meet Peter and his roommates, of which there are five. All six live in a space which is the same size as my apartment. The room is filled by bunk-beds and computer equipment; the floor littered with empty boxes of microwave noodles and dusty socks that have been trampled flat. A couple of the lads look familiar. One turns out to be a student of mine and I had previously met another – an exceptionally geeky kid with braces – at the weekly English Corner which gives eager language learners a chance to practice their oral English. Of all the hundreds of students I teach, I could probably pick out half of them in a line up. And if I've managed to commit even ten per cent of their names to memory I'd be surprised. Of course, they all know me and are always excited to see foreign teachers. They hang on our every word and take them as Gospel. Presuming I don't work at this university for the rest of my days, I'll miss this hero worship when it's gone.

The young wavy-haired student that claims to be in my writing class thanks me for giving him a good grade on his recent essay entitled 'Challenges Facing Modern China'. I had set the title as a handy way of researching what China's student intelligentsia thinks about the state of the nation. Everybody got decent results because the school advised us that the average mark should be around 85 per cent – an unthinkably generous figure by Irish standards. The essays revealed considerable awareness of China's myriad challenges but they all had the same concluding paragraph. They warned of growing inequality, overpopulation, environmental catastrophe, inflation and the danger of selling the nation's soul to capitalism. Regardless of how stark a picture was painted, the vast majority of students toed the line by dropping in a final paragraph which went something like: 'Luckily, our government has launched effective new policies to deal with this matter.'

Note that all government policies can immediately be described as 'effective' even if they were only rolled out a fortnight ago. That really is lucky.

Peter gets a call to say the basketball and football courts are open for business so we cut the chitchat and make for the stairs. I'm relieved. Sitting on the end of an unmade bunk bed being quizzed by six overly keen students is not my ideal way to spend a Sunday morning. In fairness to the lads, I'd say the same about any waking activity.

The fifty metre green football pitch is covered with the kind of artificial grass that guarantees to remove a layer of skin and leave you with an oozing burn if you are unfortunate enough to lose your footing on its slippery surface. Its beady, black sand finds its way between your toes and weighs down your runners.

As we sort out the teams – it's six against seven – we are all working under the same misconception: that lanky white lads are naturally gifted football technicians. My teammates take turns calling me by the names of marginally more gifted footballers. 'Beckham', 'Van Nistelrooy', 'Rooney', 'Ronaldo', they say in turn. It's the same joke but it seems to get funnier each time, at least as far as they are concerned.

We kick-off and the ball is immediately toed in my direction. I feign to pass but instead step over the ball, allowing it to run on to a teammate standing directly behind me. 'Ooooh,' say impressed players on both teams. Without even kicking a ball, I have become a football legend.

In my bleary-eyed delirium, I've bought into my own publicity. I feel like spraying cross-field balls all over the pitch and picking defence-splitting passes. I reckon I could shimmy past the opposition on a solo run and dribble around the keeper without breaking a sweat. I'm Johnny Giles, I'm Liam Brady, I'm Diego Maradona.

The truth is I'm a poor man's Gary Neville. Except that he's fitter, more disciplined and has superior technical ability. And he's better in the air. I stopped playing at anything close to a serious level when I was twenty. Our local side's greatest glory came when we were hammered 5-0 by Shelbourne's semi-professional apprentices in the Under-19 Cup Final. It was humiliating but we got free polo-shirts with the club crest on them. We looked the part, at least until the whistle blew.

Back then, my best bet for landing a place in the starting eleven was to target positions where competition was low. And so it was that I became a somewhat reliable, if uninventive, right-full back. Today, though, I'm the lynchpin of our six-man outfit. I'm covering every blade of artificial grass like Roy Keane in his heyday.

After five high octane minutes, I'm knackered. 'You are tired Nisterooy?' bellows a teammate. Because Chinese is a tonal language, I'm not sure how to detect sarcasm, but I wouldn't blame him if he was taking the piss. So I wheel out Excuse Number One: 'I climbed the Great Wall yesterday so I'm feeling a little stiff.'

Students here don't have much to do with their spare time so they play basketball, football and table tennis morning, noon and night. They are fit as fleas. Their skill level isn't bad either. What I can't understand is why China is so hopeless at international football. The national team has never managed to recapture the glory days of the late 1990s when they briefly found themselves ranked number thirty-seven in the world. These days they are barely in the top 100. China has the largest pool of potential players to choose from, even if football must compete with ping pong and computer games for the attention of the next generation. Just as they have cracked the economic development nut, they must surely come to dominate world football. However, I seem to recall similar predictions about US soccer.

As the game wears on and I wonder where my second wind is when I need it, I begin to realise why I might be so badly out of breath and why China won't worry Brazil, Italy and Argentina when the World Cup Finals roll around. Despite not inconsiderable skill, my new friends' tactics are naive and outdated. Every ball is kicked long and we all chase after it like a swarm of bees. It's a scene from the North Dublin Under-9 League. The notion of playing a short pass along the deck to a nearby teammate just doesn't appeal. Every aimless ball creates a fifty-fifty situation, making the odds of stringing a chain of passes together and scoring a goal quite slim. There's no time to put your foot on the ball and pick a pass.

Excuse Number Two: 'The style of game in China doesn't suit me.'

Having started with a total of thirteen players, we now have around twenty-four. You can't reserve the football court so anybody is entitled to join in. One by one, new players arrive and join the pack of busy bees hacking at the poor defenceless ball in the vicinity of the centre circle.

There are no jerseys, bibs or other identifiers so it's getting a little confusing. I can remember which players were on my side at the beginning but it is now completely impossible. I'm passing to lads who are against me and tackling my own comrades.

Excuse Number Three: 'There are too many players and I don't know who's on my team.'

I recognise one of the newest arrivals as Li Jiang, a student of mine who likes to throw verbal curveballs at me at the end of every class. It's like he spends the week dreaming up ever more bizarre questions to fire at the only foreigner he has ever meet. In his mind, I represent about five billion people, which is to say the entire population of the world outside China. Teachers in Chinese schools are not supposed to espouse political, religious or otherwise interesting viewpoints. So I'm quite the slippery politician when it comes to giving obtuse answers to straight questions.

'What do foreigners think about Japan? In China we remember the monstrous things they did in Nanjing, but do you like Japan?'

'Well, it's an interesting question ... different countries have different relationships ... it's certainly a modern country ... perhaps the US remembers Pearl Harbour ... overall there would be mixed views.'

Chinese people have trouble forgetting the series of atrocities visited upon them by their neighbours and it's a source of great annoyance that the Japanese are seen as an advanced western-style democracy while Red China has been the poor relation until very recently.

'Are you a communist?'

'Well, there's a question. I mean, you know, I'm not terribly political. Maybe it didn't work in Russia ... I can see the merit in the Chinese system. It's not perfect, of course ... but nothing is.'

That, my friend, is the perfect answer. Whatever about me being a communist, it would be more interesting to ask the Chinese whether *they* are truly still communists. But that's a question I'll hold back on until the end of term.

'Are you a Christian?'

'Well, I certainly was once ... ehm ... these days I'm not religious at all but I appreciate the moral teachings of Christianity. It's a matter of personal choice of course.'

Jesus H Christ, it can get tricky. Communism has generally been viewed as incompatible with spiritual faith and it is only very recently that the Party has become more tolerant of religion. The message had been that if you need somebody to worship, turn to Mao. But that line is softening.

Li Jiang is a Christian and he's not the only one. Around 10,000 people are baptised every day in China. This may eventually come to trouble the authorities if they see religion as a direct threat to their 'harmonious society'. There are about 80 million Christians here, accounting for seven per cent of the population. Compare that with 73 million members of the Communist Party and it's easy to imagine a return of curbs on religious freedoms.

Li Jiang tells me his favourite book is the Bible and enjoys quoting it in his essays. He loves a good pray and is one of the few people I've met here who knows Christmas was once more than just a gift swapping festival. He can even tell the difference between Jesus Christ and Santa Claus which is more than can be said of his compatriots. I've yet to see it with my own eyes, but I hear from several sources that there have been sightings of Santa Claus in a nativity scene in central Beijing. He allegedly sits behind Mary amongst the wise men. Jesus and Santa are relatively new icons for the Chinese. Both wear beards, are decent to children and come with oodles of mythology. I must watch out for St Nick nailed to crosses at Easter.

I revert to the anonymous comfort of the right-full position in an effort to avoid the ball. While I reflect on how good-tempered the game has been, Li Jiang is unceremoniously creamed by a stocky, greying man wearing heavy-duty football boots. The big guy is also wearing shin-guards. He seems to be the only one ready for battle and Li Jiang is not his first victim of the afternoon. Naturally, Jiang forgives his attacker immediately – because he's Christian and because he'd be killed if a fight broke out – and the play is waved on by consensus. There's an absence of malice despite the hectic and dogged nature of the Chinese tackle.

I haven't put in a tackle in twenty minutes for fear of overexerting myself. Part of the reason I'm failing to perform is that taking deep breaths of polluted air is not helping my lungs to recover from my early exertions.

And so we come to Excuse Number Four: 'The poor air quality is affecting my pulmonary system.'

Two of the opposition's newest members are in my Friday morning class. They both go by the name 'Kevin' and I've never seen them apart. They have identical haircuts, matching glasses and both are doing PhDs in ecology.

This week I gave their class a reading assignment about the Miss Artificial Beauty competition which was held in Beijing. It's a Miss World for the surgically enhanced. 'What do you think of beauty contests,' I asked. The room was divided. Almost all the girls thought it a ridiculous phenomenon that sends the wrong messages to young people. Some of the braver boys said beauty pageants are entertaining and people can do whatever they want. Fairly typical of the response you might expect elsewhere.

However, when it came time to do a role play everything that was said before suddenly flew out the window. As part of the exercise, the organiser of the Miss Artificial Beauty competition had to convince a hotelier to host the event in their five-star establishment. Playing the pageant organiser, Kevin 1's persuasive tactics were solely based on money and how publicity might help the hotel-owner's business. Kevin 2, the hotelier, accepted this line of reasoning and his only quibble was exactly how much money he'd get and whether the girls will demand a complimentary breakfast. 'What about the other social or moral objections?' I asked.

'But this is different. It's business,' came the stereo response from both Kevins. This went unchallenged by other students who appeared to agree. Even the most vocal would-be feminists took a pragmatic approach.

I tried to throw a spanner in the works by suggesting that the hotel owner's (imaginary) daughter abhors beauty pageants and will be deeply angry with her father if he accepts the request to host the competition. This doesn't faze them. 'Maybe your daughter would like to meet the celebrities?'

'No, she will not speak to me if we host the competition.'

'Maybe I'll buy her a horse.'

'Okay.'

I tell Kevin the Hotelier to at least *pretend* he has a moral objection to these pageants. But again, Kevin the Pageant Organiser is a persuasive chap. Having already offered the hotelier a truckload of money, the chance to meet famous people and a horse for his daughter, he has one more trick up his sleeve.

'I can introduce you to a beauty. I know many beauties – maybe 100 beauties. You can have one if you host the competition.'

'It is a deal!'

If the amoral Kevins are anything to go by, China's ascent to the top table of global superpowers owes much to moral pragmatism.

Cosmetic surgery, incidentally, is a booming business in Beijing. Small private clinics are springing up across the city to meet growing demand among the moneyed middle classes. Liposuction is just another luxury product to buy and sell. Collagen injections, botox, tummy-tucks and all manner of laser surgeries are en vogue. But so too is an operation to 'westernise' Asian eyes. An upper eyelid lift, known as blepharoplasty, helps achieve the coveted 'double eyelid' that is apparently highly desirable here.

The Chinese definition of beauty is very much based on looking like American pop stars. So while pasty-faced teens in the West smear fake tan on themselves to look a little less ghostly, Chinese girls are investing in whitening lotions which bleach their skin until they get that delightful Michael Jackson look.

We've been playing football for almost two hours. I lost interest at least an hour ago. A roar goes up from the opposition's goalkeeper and is returned by one of my teammates. Suddenly there's an extra edge to the tackling and the noise level rises in the centre of the swarm that has swallowed the ball. Peter kindly informs me that the old Next Goal The Winner rule will apply.

To be honest, I still can't get into the game. That second wind never came. Anyway, the low cloud cover has made it quite dull this morning and, if you couple that with my catching sand behind a contact lens in the opening stages of the game, you get:

Excuse Number Five: 'I can't see the ball or my teammates very well.'

So that's the Wall, the air, the numbers, the playing style and visibility. Did I complain about the pitch? Well, I think I'm better on grass.

I feel no great sense of victory when one of my teammates – who I thought was an opposition defender – hammers the ball home to end the game. We all shake hands and people continue to tell me what a joy it was to share a pitch with such a talented footballer as me. I want to get off that pitch as quickly as possible before I'm surrounded by curious students yet again. It's only 10.00 am so there's still plenty of time to rescue the morning by catching the tail end of the Sunday lie-in.

Yesterday's trip to the Wall, today's early morning football and the broken lift have left me exhausted. I collapse into bed next to Girlfriend who murmurs, 'How did you get on?'

I consider spinning some yarn detailing imagined glorious exploits but haven't got the energy.

'I need a holiday.'

15

Willkommen Qingdao

Masses mill around in front of Beijing Railway Station like a swarm of confused bees. And none so confused as us. Long, disorderly queues stretch out across the pedestrianised square before the building's grand 1950s facade. In a way that central train stations tend to do, the area surrounding Beijing's transportation hub has attracted an eclectic cross-section of society. Suited businessmen walk briskly at forty-five degree angles, giving the impression that they might be important; bespectacled students from the country grip the straps of their backpacks with their thumbs as they gaze up in bewildered awe at the city's skyscrapers; homeless amputees dressed in rags wearily do the rounds asking for spare change; shifty pickpockets edge towards their next victim; hopeful migrant workers lug the entire contents of their lives in hard-wearing blue and white striped carryalls; and a pair of stressed Irish tourists paw a guidebook while waiting impatiently to buy train tickets.

You can catch trains to Shanghai, Macau, Guangzhou or even Pyongyang from here if you like. We are bound for the relatively nearby city of Qingdao. It's only eight hours away.

Our travel book claims to hold all the key phrases we'll need to navigate the ticket-buying transaction. However, when it's finally our turn to approach the jaded teenager sitting behind a window in one of the ticket booths, we are yet again defeated by the fact that Chinese is a tonal language. The letters which form the words we need are all there in black and white, arranged in the correct order, but we can't seem to pronounce them in a pitch that is comprehensible to the droopy-eyed vendor. The people behind us are getting antsy, which is adding to our stress. A man with fresh scars on his face approaches from over my shoulder to offer assistance. I extend my elbows, taking him for a queue skipper. He barges through all the same and helps us buy two tickets for the night train to Qingdao.

There are four categories of ticket. 'Soft sleeper' and 'hard sleeper' are effectively beds in enclosed and open cabins respectively, while 'soft seats' and 'hard seats' are precisely what you might expect. Scarface has scored us a pair of hard seats. In all the fuss, I'm just happy to be holding two slips of card which will get us inside the station, away from the dodgy mayhem of the square. Soft sleeper, hard seat – I don't suppose it makes that much difference.

Alas, the station building houses a chaotic commuter hell, every bit as energy-sapping as the scene outside. We pass our backpacks through a scanner – which I'm sure is just a conveyor belt that rolls through an empty metal box. There's nobody watching x-ray images on a monitor; the scanner is just there to give the impression that security is tight. Public safety placebos are everywhere these days. How else to explain seatbelts on aeroplanes?

Hundreds of travellers are rushing around clutching tickets and suitcases. It looks like bedlam to me, but there's a certain organisation to the pandemonium in here. At the very least, everybody else seems to know where they are going.

Having shown our tickets to several members of staff and eventually being pointed towards Waiting Room Two, we're on an escalator where panicky passengers continue to ram their huge travel bags into our ankles as they push past. Such is the frenzied desperation with which people carry themselves in and around

Beijing Railway Station that you'd think the city was due to explode when the clock strikes midnight.

We can't understand any of the announcements booming over the tannoy, nor can we read most of what flashes up on the huge overhead information board. But we know our train's code is T-21 so we'll hang around in the stinking waiting room until we see or hear mention of it.

I'd say this is what purgatory would look like. Half-dead sinners are lying prostrate on a row of three painfully uncomfortable plastic bucket seats. Children (who should surely be in limbo) are bawling for want of food and warmth. It's home to thieves, mouchers and Irish backpackers who are trying not to inhale the bacteria-laden air for fear of catching whatever disease is making the crusty old janitor violently cough as he leans morbidly on a mop handle.

Everybody is suffering for an ill-defined period in a cold, infinitely large cavern, waiting to be invited to approach the pearly gates – except the gates here are made of wrought iron and there's no guarantee of eternal happiness on the other side.

There's a stirring as the letters on the info board roll over to announce that T-21 is ready for boarding through gate number 3. Thank you Saint Peter.

This reminds me of the scrum that ensues when a Ryanair flight is called, except there are ten times as many people swarming around the gate. The previously zombified huddled masses are suddenly fighting to be first in the queue. I can never understand such hyperactivity among mentally healthy ticket-holding adults. But what can you do, only join in?

We may have trampled on a few elderly people in the process, but we made it through the ticket-check to the relative calm on the other side of the gate. It's heaven indeed.

There's a lone man selling water and tiny fold-up seats on the platform. The seats look like foot stools, which I presume are for resting your feet while you stretch the legs out during the leisurely journey.

Stepping up into the carriage, we encounter a bottleneck as passengers battle it out in the carriage to stow their luggage overhead. Our seats are numbered though so it's just a matter of waiting for the chaos to dissipate.

But it never does. A few uncomfortable minutes later the doors are closed and a broad-shouldered stewardess, in a pristine blue uniform, forces her way through the crowd just in time for us to ask where precisely our seats are – the carriage is chockablock.

She herds us towards two groups of six seats, pointing to the tiny numbers by the window. Our seats are on opposite sides of the carriage and both are occupied by harried middle-aged men. We politely show our tickets to the squatters, who meekly accept they have got the wrong seat and make way.

The man vacating my seat is chatting with the woman opposite. She, in turn, is bringing the young girl next to her into the conversation. As I take my seat, a teenage boy with overstyled hair arrives and plonks his bag on the table. He greets the young girl merrily, prompting her to jump up brightly and give him her seat. Those who are standing continue to chat to seated passengers, initially leading me to think they are all part of the same family. But as more passengers pile into our carriage it becomes obvious that there simply are not enough seats for everyone. The train is overbooked by about thirty per cent. What's more, these people don't know one another, they are just remarkably friendly. No doubt they'd have shoved each other down a train station escalator in the heat of the Battle of the Boarding Gate, but once all are aboard, a temporary community is born.

We may have the cheapest seats on the train, but there is a ticket class which is still cheaper: standing space in the 'hard seat' carriage. It now becomes clear why there was such a roaring trade to be done in foot stools. Those who have bought the cheapest tickets of all are squatting on the tiny stools in the aisle. One particularly gaunt gent is sitting on a four stone sack of yams chewing sunflower seeds. Nobody but me cares that he's spitting shells all over the floor. We're all one big happy family here.

The teenager with salon-fresh hair is intent on making conversation with me, despite not having a word of English. He's all chat. He catches me making eyes at Girlfriend and establishes that we are together by using the crudest of hand gestures which roughly translates as, 'Are you hitting that?'. He then points at the weasel-faced acnefest-in-a-baseball-cap next to me, before pointing at Girlfriend with a questioning expression. Either he's trying to set my neighbour up with my girlfriend or he's kindly arranging for them to swap seats.

Seats are swapped. Now he has two foreigners to stare at with his silly grin. He gives me a big thumbs up to compliment me on my glasses. I compliment his hairstyle in return. Girlfriend asks if he has been speaking English with me by pointing at his mouth and then at my lips. He thinks she's suggesting a kiss and backs off a little.

We tell him in our best Chinese that we're Irish but he hasn't a clue what we're on about. So a map is drawn on the back of a paper bag. Still nothing. The man next to him points out Britain and France on our crude map of the world and our new friend acts like he has heard of Ireland before. We're not convinced. In any case, he seems highly disappointed that we aren't Americans and conversation fizzles out.

It's hard to get any sleep on a hard seat in a jam-packed train carriage which leaves its blinding lights on all night. However, not for the first time, I notice that Chinese people have evolved a useful knack for catching a few winks in the most uncomfortable positions. And in such friendly situations as these, complete strangers are lying on each other's shoulders and leaning into one another for warmth and support. It's camaraderie, it's trust, it's China.

The chatty guy opposite is asleep with his head on the table and there's a young girl on the floor nestling her head into the crook of my leg while the generously proportioned woman in the aisle relaxes onto my shoulder. Communism is pretty cosy.

As much as we're enjoying the experience, it is agreed that we are definitely booking into a decent hotel on arrival in Qingdao. The novelty of it all wears off after a couple of wakeful hours as we realise how filthy the train is. We're the only ones even mildly perturbed when several cockroaches sprint up the wall and across the table. Our disgust is a source of some amusement to our train buddies.

Given that moving from our seats would mean climbing over a mound of bodies, there no chance of visiting the probably-horrible toilet which can be smelled but not seen from any seat in the carriage. It's best if we just take off our glasses, close our eyes and pretend we're not in a cuboid cesspit.

Of course slumber remains a pipe dream. Sleep is one of those things where the harder you try, the less likely you are to succeed. We manage to wake up a dozen people when Girlfriend mistakes a label on the side of my t-shirt for a cockroach. I try to flick it off but it won't budge. Before we know it, we're on our feet frantically brushing the side of my shirt and shouting 'Jeezus!' which is met with a chorus of laughter that refuses to die down for several minutes, even after we put on our glasses and realise what we've been doing.

Embarrassed, we resign ourselves to a sleepless night and stare out the window at the uninspiring but nonetheless fascinating landscape which has been illuminated by the early morning sun.

The scenery is greener than expected. It's just past 5.00 am and there are people out working the fields. We pass by villages where families have been suffocated by generations of poverty, but it's a far from hopeless picture. Several built-up towns are home to rows of abandoned apartment buildings waiting to be bulldozed.

100 yards away are shiny new apartment blocks with washing flapping in the breeze on taut balcony clotheslines. The roads may be dust tracks and shanty shacks litter the outskirts of town but there are signs of hope. In other towns, people still live in the dilapidated towers waiting for their new homes to be unveiled from their shrouds of green gauze. Not every hamlet knows of progress but most of those who are toiling at 5.15 am feel like times are changing.

I'm reminded of the answer I gave colleagues at the university when asked why I came to China. All that guff about it being an exciting time to be in a country undergoing such a dramatic transformation seems to make more sense by the day. I'm beginning to believe my own bullshit.

Our approach to travel planning is based on flicking through guide books, the cursory browsing of websites and a belief that anywhere remotely near the coast is worth a visit. And so we find ourselves in Qingdao. We are taking the long way to Shanghai in the hope of getting to know China beyond the big cities. We could have flown directly to Shanghai, taken a few snaps and hopped back on a plane but we would have missed out on the mayhem, the insomnia and the cockroaches.

Qingdao has plenty to recommend it. This is where Beijingers go on holiday. Its beaches are reputably among the best in northern China; its thriving central business district hosts a fair share of sky-scraping office towers; and it was selected to host the sailing events during the Beijing Olympics. From here we can also take in a handful of the Shandong Province's smaller cities – although 'small' is a relative term in China.

The population of the greater Qingdao area is over seven million, with more than 2.5 million living in the city. I'll be honest and say that I'd never heard of the place until a few months ago. China boasts eighteen of the world's 100 biggest cities – twice as many as the US – although after Shanghai, Beijing and Hong Kong, most of us would struggle to name them. Of the forty-nine cities with more than one million people, I doubt most Chinese could name the top twenty.

With so many megacities, is it any wonder that the teenager on the train had never heard of little old Ireland? China's on a different scale to the rest of the world.

We emerge from the train station to find none of the swanky office blocks or beachside promenades promised by the guide book. Instead, we're in a grimy side street surrounded by twenty unhinged touts offering hotels, taxis, maps, and tacky knickknacks. The stench of open bins is enough to make you want to get back on a train, and the mob that are pulling and shouting at us make it difficult to get our bearings. Spitting seems to be en vogue here too.

It's a little after 7.00 am. We're tired. We haven't slept in twenty-four hours and the last eight hours have been spent squashed into a corner breathing the recycled air of our fellow passengers. We feel deserving of a little pampering so we scan down the list of four hotels we have scribbled on a scrap of paper – the fruits of an earlier internet search – and choose the four-star Dong Feng Hotel. One night on a Chinese economy class cattle cart brings out the mollycoddled westerners in us. We're pining for cleanliness, comfort and air-conditioning.

A fleet of motorised three-wheelers with wooden boxes built onto their back seats line up waiting for business behind a row of taxis. Too tired to care for our personal safety, we hop in the back of a three-wheeler and point to the name of the road we wish we were on.

The driver is a sour-faced old grumbler with wispy grey hairs on his chin. He asks for 30 kuai and we couldn't be arsed haggling. Just get us out of this nightmare please Wispy.

He revs the engine for three long minutes before pulling out in front of the first taxi I've seen take a fare. It's like he was waiting for something to come along the road before taking off. Despite the incredible noise of our engine, the fact that we are overtaken by a pedestrian pushing a pram suggests this is not a high performance vehicle. The driver turns the engine off on the way down hills to save petrol as I begin to wonder whether this machine is really just a modified lawnmower. These spluttering little motor-trikes must be responsible for half the pollution in Qingdao.

Our chauffeur is a born risk taker. He drives like a man who long ago gave up on life and would happily have it all ended by a lorry. Our hearts are in our mouths as he wildly overestimates his ability to make it across four lanes of traffic at 6 mph. All other road users are beeping at us but the driver fixes his gaze straight ahead. To hell with the lot of them. He keeps cutting across on-coming traffic but is outraged when a taxi does the same to him. If nothing else, the kamikaze jaunt has woken us up.

Chugging up a gentle hill, spitting out thick plumes of leaded smoke while swaying left and right on a busy motorway, the driver points to a road sign and pulls over. Out we get. We're shaken and stirred but glad to be almost at the hotel. Or so we think.

Staring blankly through our map, we begin to realise that the road on which our hotel is located is exceptionally long. We could be close or it might be half an hour's walk away – in either direction.

Having been besieged by predators at the train station, I'm a little wary when three people stop to offer help: a lightly-bearded motorcyclist, a teenage girl and a middle-aged woman. The motorcyclist knows the name of the hotel and with a little help from the schoolgirl with pigtails and swotty glasses, they tell us how to get there. Better still, the older woman suggests we follow her as she lives in that general direction. She hasn't a word of English, apart from a mangled 'Welcome to China', but she's still altogether charming. Big rosy cheeks and crooked-toothed smile, she brings us all the way to the hotel, even though it's a quarter of a mile past her home. We know which house is hers because she stops off to drop in her fruit and veg and returns with two umbrellas, insisting that we accept one of them as a gift. It's not raining; she just wants us to remember Qingdao as having friendly locals. Done.

It's only 8.00 am but we manage to check into the pristine Dong Feng immediately. This is the earliest I've ever been let into a hotel. We shower to wash away the memory of the train journey before collapsing into a huge king size bed with crisp white sheets, tucked tightly under a firm but fair mattress.

We sleep until about 4.00 pm when I'm awakened by the sound of Girlfriend's stomach rumbling. We don't know whether it's time for breakfast, lunch or dinner so we share a bar of chocolate and an apple, then grab roast corns on the cob from a street stall while exploring the city.

The paved promenade by the seafront is the main attraction in a city that has a distinctly European flavour. Qingdao was governed by Germany from 1897 to 1914 and the Teutonic influence is to the fore in the city's architecture. Universities, churches and, most significantly, a brewery, answer the Pythonesque question, 'What have the Germans ever done for us?'

Despite the obvious German imprint, the Chinese call Qingdao 'China's Switzerland'. That's probably just a two fingers to the old colonial master.

Tsingtao beer is famous across China and tastes just like a blonde German brew, except that it's a little watery. And, of course, it's incredibly cheap. Holidaymakers lap it up by the seafront as the afternoon slowly passes and we adjust to the wonderfully slower pace.

Strolling along the imaginatively titled Qingdao Bathing Beach No. 1, I'm disappointed by the quality of the coarse stony sand.

The sudsy sewage sloshing against the rocks does nothing to make you want a paddle. Don't ask me why, but I notice that all female bathers are in one-piece swimsuits and there's a strong preference for wearing shorts or sarongs over togs. I hadn't got the Chinese pegged as a prudish people but thongs and string bikinis are one aspect of German culture that has not been absorbed by Qingdao.

Oh wait, there's a woman in a two-piece getting out of the water – the floozy!

The precious guide book suggests we try Bathing Beach No. 2 as the sand is allegedly better and it's less crowded. En route, we spot a bride and groom posing for pictures in the sand dunes. It's a real live photo shoot, complete with a photographer, an art director with make-up bags, and a fresh-faced assistant angling a giant sheet of aluminium foil to get the lighting just right. Ten yards on, we happen across another bride strutting to the top of a sandy peak to have her photo taken. Hang on, there's a third bride. And another one. And another. In 100 square metres of sand dune we count nine brides with full makeup and impractically extravagant hairdos. On the damp sand below, a photographer is directing bride number ten into a playful pose, featuring feigned laughter, as his assistant rushes in to touch up the bride's blush between shots.

These kinds of prenuptial photo opportunities are all the rage and Qingdao is a popular spot for moneyed Beijingers. In many cases, the couple doesn't actually get married for several months. Brides-to-be get dolled up in rented frocks and lie in the sand looking girly, while their bored grooms kick stones around waiting until the whole ordeal is over. It's all about the brides. And it's big business. Companies offering hair, makeup, dress rental and photography are raking it in. We have half a mind to rent a dress, a suit and a snapper and mail the photos home for a laugh. But we're getting hungry.

My ongoing failure to grasp the sprawling scale of small Chinese cities has led us to walk miles from afternoon into evening, stopping only so I can frown at the map and say, 'According to this it should be just a little further on'.

It's getting dark by the time we make it to Yunxiao lu on the east side of the city. The road is part of a network of busy little streets around which domineering temples of glass and steel have grown into the economic engine room of what looks like a rather chic town by night. We walk its full length before settling on a popular spot which displays its food in transparent plastic boxes on a tiered countertop so patrons can select their dinner by hand. The waiter talks us into ordering a special fish dish and we pick some fried pork just in case the fish is unpalatable.

There's a photo of Kim Jong-il on the wall, apparently enjoying dinner in this very restaurant. The Chinese have a rather ambiguous attitude to the country they call the Democratic People's Republic of Korea. For one thing, North Korea is a communist state and the neighbouring comrades have been brothers-in-arms. For another, China discourages the international community from laying into Kim Jong-il because Beijing prefers to push the line that the US and company shouldn't interfere with the affairs of sovereign nations. They don't want regime change or democracy foisted on Pyongyang for fear that the West might encourage the democratisation of China. At the same time, North Korea is an embarrassment to communists. It's an economic basket case where people are starved of food and basic freedoms. Still, looking at the picture of Kim Jong-il tucking into a lump of fried cow, you wouldn't think he had a care in the world. I suppose *he* doesn't.

The meal is decent, though not exceptional – the fish is a little bony. But we wash it down with a few bottles of the local brew and life seems good again. We pay up a modest sum and hit the road where taxis slow down and honk at us to advertise their services. We take one of them up on their offer and head back across the city. I hop in the front and pull the distressingly dusty seatbelt around me. There's nowhere to clip it. If it has ever been used, it must have been a very long time ago. The slippery-faced taxi driver gestures dismissively and laughs as if to say, 'Don't be silly, Big Nose, you won't be needin' that here'. He floors it. We overtake people, cut across cars and buses, break red lights and make it home in four minutes. I have a good mind to give him a stern lecture on road safety when we screech to a halt on the ramp outside the hotel. But I haven't the energy. Instead I give him 13 kuai and a hearty 'xie xie', which hopefully means thanks.

The hotel probably deserves at least three of its four stars. But there are one or two things that are beginning to look a little odd. There's a sign on the doorknob which reads: 'For your safety, when other guests knock at your door, please don't open. If you have some problems dial 2134. The Security Department will help you.'

I bet the security crowd are just uniformed pimps. There's a separate note by the bedside which says, amongst other more run-of-the-mill pleasantries: 'Don't open the door for strangers and don't let the strangers come into your room.'

I had read a review of the altogether plusher and pricier Crowne Plaza Hotel down the road which said it would have been a great spot if it weren't for the fact that the hotel bar is effectively a brothel. I'm fully expecting somebody to come a-knockin' sooner or later.

'Darling, did you order a prostitute?'

The bathroom features a '3-in-1' shampoo/conditioner/shower gel dispenser. Presumably they hadn't the funds to provide separate bottles of each. Or maybe there was no room left on the bathroom shelf after they'd stocked up on essentials like: a vibrating condom, his 'n' hers genital wash, two packs of Chinese medicinal preparations claiming to 'enhance sexuality and energy', and a compressed towel which promises to expand to ten times its size when placed in water.

I'm wondering whether this hotel turns into an all-out whorehouse on the stroke of midnight. It's 11:20 pm. I'm battening down the hatches.

The shocking thing about the Chinese 'medicinal' genital wash is its guarantee of protection against sexually transmitted infections. I can't read the ingredients – they're in Chinese – but I bet it's just spiced alcohol rub or scented massage oil making promises it can't keep: 'As a pure Chinese medicinal preparation it can quickly kill any kinds of latent germs and pathogens. It can prevent cross infection effectively and won't cause dependency.'

It goes on to advise that the company's other products should also be purchased and used before and after intercourse. Good clean sex is big business.

It comes as a bit of a let down that nobody bothers us all night. Instead, I'm woken around 4.30 am by severe abdominal discomfort which sends me racing for the bathroom. Let's skip the details. Suffice it to say that I blame that weird fish dish for my current condition. And that I made the same mad dash twice more before dawn.

My funny tummy is no laughing matter when the next day we make our way to Zhanshan Temple, a mountainside Buddhist enclave high above Qingdao's coastline. As fascinating as the temple is, my mind is far too busy to achieve nirvana, as I'm totally focused on finding a toilet. I have no interest in desecrating a religious site but if a bathroom doesn't present itself very soon, I'll have to run the risk of angering Buddha. And probably the monks.

Fortunately for all concerned, a suitable facility is found in the nick of time. It may be just a wooden cubicle badly built around a hole in the ground but it relieves the threat of embarrassment and I'm free to enjoy the scene.

Now, where was I? Ah yes, the monks.

The monks say little but they're not shy about charging us in to see their performance. We've already paid into the park and coughed up another few kuai for a cable car to get to this point. Maybe monks are capitalists.

It's strange that the government treats these robed holy men with such suspicion, as if their lifestyle fails to fit in with the communist ideal. The monks' mini-community is the closest thing to pure communism I've seen since arriving in China – notwithstanding the admission fee. While the rest of China is wrapping itself up in consumerism, the Buddhists here have few possessions; they eat humble meals and exist without the warm glow of LCD televisions and gas-fired central heating.

There are several temples interspersed among long dormitories and dining halls. Large orange robes adorn washing lines, strung across a courtyard between ornate red huts. Pagodas, classrooms and temples are all open to inspection. There's a group of rough-looking workers guffawing and smoking while they take an extended break from laying new concrete slabs outside the classroom. They are spoiling the scene.

Turning a corner, it transpires we are just in time for the evening prayer. Inside a large temple, there is a serene statue of Buddha before whom fresh fruit has been laid. A giant gong hangs from a ceiling which is hand-painted in intricate patterns of blue and green.

A deep, solemn drum is thumped by a slight, young monk in a robe so crisp it makes me suspect he owns a travel iron. He thumps the drum again. There's nothing but the sound of twenty silent monks shuffling barefoot on floorboards. Thump. Silence. Thump.

An older, glazed monk strikes up a haunting chant as a small but powerful bell is sounded. The young monks, some still in their teens, answer in unison like an orchestra of double basses. It's hypnotic. If you could buy robes here I'd shave my head and sell my shoes in a flash just so I could join in.

Every few minutes, one of the rookies steps out to have a spit. One lad cleared his nose with a serious snort then unleashed a throatload of phlegm on the step outside before popping back in and slipping into the chanting.

The evening chant-along lasts about an hour. We get so wrapped up in the show that we miss the cable car home and have to make our own way out of the park. Fortunately, there's always a steady supply of young trendies floating in our general direction hoping to be asked for help. We're very obliging in that regard. And so it is that two overexcited students tell us which bus to get, while giggling through their hands and apologising for having imperfect English.

A quiet drink and a safe snack at the hotel restaurant are in order before an early night. We need a little rest because tomorrow we are headed to another of China's small towns: Yantai, a city home to over six million people which I hadn't heard of until last Thursday.

Whoever said it was a small world had obviously never been to China.

16

Massaging HJV Figures

'Hell-lo?'

'Massagey?'

'Ehm, no. No, thanks. Xie xie (thanks).'

'Massagey, ok?'

'Bu yao (don't want). Zaijian (goodbye).'

'Another prostitute?' asks Girlfriend while casually rummaging through a rucksack wondering why we packed so few pairs of socks. 'Yeah – sounded like the one in the blonde wig,' I reply with parallel nonchalance, glued to the ads on CNN.

We say nothing for a few moments before turning to look at each other with bemused grins. When did phone calls from whores stop being a talking point?

We're sitting in a seedy hotel in Yantai built in the style of the old Ballymun flats. The bathroom is crammed with magic sex lotions; there are erotic TV channels available on demand; the bedside locker hides spare boxer shorts wrapped in cellophane; and our room comes complete with an 'L' shaped faux leather sofa and an irreparably stained coffee table. The off-white couch is either old, dirty or both, and features half a dozen holes which, if the room were bright enough, could probably be confirmed as cigarette burns. Fortunately, there's a dimmer switch so the lights can be dipped down real low if the grime is ruining the romance.

There are posters in the lobby advertising the basement massage parlour which is staffed by heavily made-up but scantily dressed ladies who appear to be permanently on the brink of falling off their very high heels on the way down the stairs.

What a place! All we can do is laugh and wonder how on earth our lives went from a comfortably dull, office-based existence in Dublin to the excitingly filthy normality we now take in our stride in China.

It's teeming down. I haven't seen a drop of rain in weeks. But now, as we haul our rucksacks out of a taxi's boot beside a bus stop, the heavens have opened.

Qingdao has been good to us for a couple of days but it's time to discover the charms of Yantai, a burgeoning port city a little further up the coast. First, though, we must deal with a noisy band of locals roaring things in our direction that we don't understand while a wall of water moistens our bones.

When engaged by excitable strangers I always presume they want money and put my hands on my pockets. On, mind, not in. The pockets on my khaki pants are buttoned shut, reflecting my own lack of openness to the unfamiliar.

I wave them away, frowning, and we take shelter from the heavy downpour under a footbridge where we can contemplate our next move. As we shake off the excess water and realise that we don't know what time or from where our bus leaves, a strong-looking girl in her twenties approaches in full animation. She's wearing a black t-shirt fronted by a giant, silver Playboy bunny and gets understandably agitated by my refusal to acknowledge her presence. She pucks me in the arm, insisting that we follow her. Entirely convinced she's on the make, I just stare past her muttering, 'Don't so much as look at her' out of the side of my mouth. Girlfriend isn't as uptight as me, readily revealing that we were going to Yantai. The Playboy Girl seems like she couldn't care less where we are headed and she urges us to board a bus ten feet away. I'm highly reluctant, but my trusting partner is already pursuing the potential mugger up the stairs of the coach. No point taking cover under a bridge like a lone, drenched troll. And anyway, Girlfriend has all our cash in her bum-bag, so I follow the money.

I step tentatively onto the bus, which is populated by half a dozen passengers. There's no driver but the engine is running. I sit in the driver's seat, ostensibly for the laugh but secretly because it's the seat nearest the door. Girlfriend is chatting to a young pair of art students who have a smattering of English and look a little concerned for us. 'This is not the bus to Yantai,' confides the oddly priggish girl who says she's studying painting.

The Playboy Girl has summoned a posse of menacing-looking characters to come gawk at us and is now forcefully encouraging the artsy couple not to frighten us away by mentioning that this is really the bus to god-knows-where.

The posse is taking baby steps, edging ever closer to me with wide eyes and twitchy smiles. They look like thirsty zombies ready to pounce but fearful of frightening away the prey. I have a horrible feeling that we've just been ushered into a mobile mugging den. The guy with the gold teeth looks capable of demanding all our worldly goods as a toll for letting us safely back down the steps of the bus.

As the uncomfortable minutes tick past, I begin to wonder why they don't just rob us and be done with it. They are fascinated by us, and our watches. One cross-eyed gent with matted hair offers to buy my watch which had been a present from former work friends. I politely decline his kind offer, even though he has produced a roll of one kuai notes. He keeps looking at it and pointing to show others. There are, at this stage, about a dozen people on board, although there's a constant turnover with some characters hopping on and off every two minutes to shout at passersby.

The guy obsessing about my watch is making me uneasy. He hasn't spoken a word of English up to this point but slowly looks up at me and says, quietly and most sincerely, 'beautiful', before returning his gaze to my chunky time piece. It's a nice watch, but he is in such breathtaken awe that you'd think he'd just seen the Mona Lisa up close.

Once ten minutes pass without violence or larceny, my suspicious mind begins to settle and I get into the groove of the exuberant banter provided by our hosts.

We tell the art students we are leaving Qingdao for Yantai and, pointing at our map, ask them to recommend other cities in the Shandong province that might be worth a look. 'Qingdao,' they say in unison without batting an eyelid. 'Qingdao is the most beautiful city in all of China.' We come up against this regularly, especially when teaching. Ask a Chinese person to recommend a place of interest and they are incapable of offering a suggestion beyond their hometown – even when you're waiting for a bus to take you out of the place.

As the wannabe painter hands us a bar of Galaxy chocolate as a gift, our gold-toothed friend comes running frantically back up the steps of the bus. 'Yantai! Yantai!'

In all the fear and fun we had taken our eye off the ball and nearly missed our bus out of town. Luckily, Goldie had our backs. He and an accomplice have flagged down the bus in the middle of the road and are refusing to let it move until we are safely on board. Our Qingdao posse laugh and wave giddily as we tear off down a narrow road towards the expressway.

It turns out the Playboy Girl only wanted us on board the bus for the craic rather than to fleece us. Maybe my paranoia is misplaced in China; maybe it stands in the way of new experiences. Or maybe that's just the kind of thinking that leaves you open to predators.

The bus driver is a horn-happy nut job. He must be the lunatic brother of the real driver, out on temporary release from a community psychiatry facility. The qualified, sane sibling probably has his feet up by Beach No. 2.

The madman's hooting his honker at everybody while drifting into the centre of the road, forcing oncoming traffic to swerve. It would make him unhappy if he didn't have a pair of wheels either side of the broken white line that bisects the street. And we don't want to see him unhappy.

He's muttering constantly and shouting sporadically, making gestures that suggest he reckons everyone else is off their rocker. 'Oh they're all out today,' he's thinking.

The only other explanation for his behaviour is that, firstly, he's deaf and doesn't realise that his thumb is holding down the horn. And secondly, he's quite drunk.

Regardless of whether he's barmy or just a deaf drunk, there's not a thing I can do from the discomfort of my worn draylon bus seat, so I fix my eyes on the Jackie Chan film that's showing on a small TV perched on a bracket in the corner above the driver's head. For an old rust bucket of a twenty-seat bus that must have fifteen years' service under its fan belt, the onboard entertainment is a welcome surprise. Still more astonishing is that the movie is subtitled in English. The subtitles trail the pictures by a full ten seconds but it's better than the tinny radio that comes as standard on most Chinese coach services.

We survive the trip and set about orientating ourselves on the greyscale streets of Yantai. The locals are friendly but nobody has heard of the hotel that we have booked online. And, not for the first time, the language barrier is our greatest enemy. My grandfather used to say, 'You'll never be lost, so long as you've a tongue in your head'. With all due respect to Granda Finnegan, I don't think he ever made it to China.

We walk hopefully towards the centre of town, happy to explore. Rambling around Yantai, you get a snapshot of what's happening in medium-sized cities up and down the east of China. It's under construction. You wouldn't be shocked to see signs telling foreigners they've caught Yantai at a bad time and asking that they come back in 2015 when things are really roaring.

Street after street, the half-finished city presents spanking new office blocks next to frighteningly dilapidated housing towers. Swish boutiques, untroubled by customers, sit next to busy neighbourhood grocers. Ten yards on, there's a gaping, dusty cavity where an old building has lately been demolished. Construction workers are erecting hoarding which advertises the new plaza that will fill the gap. The eight foot boards are full of photographs of smiling westerners superimposed onto a computer-generated impression of plush modern offices.

Buildings here are of three varieties: the very old, the very new and the half-built. It's like nothing has been built in China for sixty years and they are desperate to make amends with a frenzied five-year construction programme.

The people are similarly divisible. The twenty-somethings strut confidently about town. They have known nothing but progress and are maturing at a time of plenty.

The older generation look a little bewildered. Mao, their hero, is still on all the banknotes and his wise words are quoted *ad nauseum,* but are coffee shops and department stores the ultimate destination of the communist revolution?

Those of middle age know more of Mao the myth than Mao the man. Deng Xiaoping, the pro-market reformer of the 1980s, is their idol and it's they who are reaping the benefits of economic growth. The struggle to define 'Socialism with Chinese Characteristics' seems far from their minds as they sit behind the wheel of German saloons.

We find our hotel, decline a massage, and continue the exploration unburdened by backpacks. There's a sea breeze whistling through Nan Dajie, a main thoroughfare lined with offices and shops. We stop at a temple which is so out of place that it looks as though it were dropped here accidentally from above by a careless giant. It is surrounded by twenty-storey office towers – some very old, but mostly very new – and is the only low rise building in sight. A plaque on the wall reads 'Yantai Museum'. This demands further investigation.

The stillness inside suggests visitors might be studying the exhibits in respectful silence, but the truth is that there are no visitors. In fact, we have to wait several minutes for a surprised member of staff to arrive so we can pay the 10 kuai entry fee. Honest eejits, are we not?

It is typically overstaffed for such a tiny place. The staff are exceptionally courteous, perhaps because they don't get too many punters on quiet Tuesday afternoons. Whatever the reason, they have yet to develop the contempt for tourists that's usually required for museum ushers.

The temple itself is beautiful – freshly refurbished with lead paint, no doubt. Very little English is available in the museum but the artifacts speak for themselves. Alas, many have been retouched and, in some cases, entirely remodelled in plaster. Sitting in dim glass cases are cooking pots and weapons from what we would broadly call the middle ages, but China breaks down into several periods based on which dynasty ran the show at the time.

It's amazing how civilisations, separated by thousands of miles, come up with almost identical solutions to everyday problems like cooking and killing.

A bucktoothed usher sits beside the remains of a tiny wooden boat which, if it had washed up on Ireland's western shore, would be labelled 'currach' and displayed in a Dublin museum. I smile pensively at the usher while thinking that our ancestors were probably even more alike than we are now, despite globalisation. She smiles back, probably wondering why I'm being so creepy.

It takes just half an hour to see the museum so we do a second lap just to get value for money. With that out of the way, it's back to the hotel where we will prepare for dinner by watching CNN while debating whether it's best to mosey about town until a decent restaurant reveals itself or to resort to the supposed safety of the guidebook. We feel like we should take our chances with a random local restaurant but we tried that in Qingdao and got food poisoning so I want to err on the side of caution. Dinner is a serious matter.

No sooner have we turned on the television than the phone rings. I answer and, yet again, it's the madam from the 'Massagey' parlour in the basement. I still don't want a massage, although my shoulder blades are a little tense from the rucksack.

Five minutes later, there is a knock at the door. Telemarketing is one thing, but door-to-door sex sales is a bit much. I convince Girlfriend to answer the knock just to make it clear to the eager masseuses that my answer isn't going to change, but by the time she does so, the caller has moved on – perhaps frightened away by the sound of another female voice. We decide to take our dinner debate to the streets where we'll be safe from offers of cheap sex.

Darkness has fallen abruptly as we whiled away half an hour in the internet cafe next to our hotel. An online search for dinner options was the compromise between random roaming and relying on Lonely Planet researchers. We've found just the place but it will require a taxi ride.

Walking towards the better-lit seafront promenade, we take a turn down Chaoyang Jie – a shady road lined with neon-smothered shop fronts and kerb-side bars. The walls are covered with mobile phone numbers for services unspecified. Our map suggests this place is a main thoroughfare but our guts say something different.

The streetlamps are out, leaving the muted glow of bar lights as the only aid to pedestrians struggling to pick their way through the rubble strewn across the street. A recent demolition has left lumps of brick and plaster on what has become a pitch black walkway.

Along with being punched in the nose, stubbing one's toe tops the list of the most infuriating sensations available to humans. It incites decent folk to use rude words they only ever hear on rap albums. Still, there is one major plus to walking down a blacked-out alley in China with a raging, swollen toe: it's strangely safe. I can't imagine walking at night down a street in a western city – where you can't see your own feet – without a justifiable fear of attack.

Despite my tendency to effect a wall of paranoia when strangers come within two metres, there's no threat of violent crime in China, no sense of malice. Pickpockets, con artists and watch-snatchers, yes, but in-your-face-with-a-Stanley-blade holdups are not their style.

Emerging from the veritable tunnel that was Chaoyang Jie, we swing a right onto the gleaming new tiles spread across the esplanade above the shore. Beams from innumerate space-age lamps illuminate the pristine path with a dazzling glare. I imagine they've installed twice as many lights as necessary because the eco-friendly lamps only use half the energy.

Locals and holidaymakers – all of whom are Chinese – are enjoying an evening constitutional before dinner. It could be a re-vamped Spanish coastal resort, without the vomiting 18-30s and disgruntled residents.

In the space of 100 yards, we have taken in a quasi-brothel, a smart internet cafe, a few seedy bars, a demolition site, and a thriving holiday hotspot. In China, you never know what's around the next corner.

A dozen beds staffed by men and women in white line the path by a makeshift taxi rank. It's a flashback to images of hospital trolleys in the car parks of Irish A&E departments. But these are, in fact, massage tables. And the staff are genuine massage technicians. There's no special services, no 'finish', just upper body muscle manipulation. Perhaps the only way to practice as a masseuse without your neighbours presuming that you are a de facto sex worker is to conduct your business in public.

A taxi takes us on a circuitous ten minutes' journey to Jackie's Restaurant, only for us to find we should have made a reservation. The exceptionally friendly and xenophilic staff say we may amuse ourselves at the bar until a table becomes available. We've no plan B and Jackie's serves imported European beers so we pull up a couple of bar stools, order some strong Belgian ale and feast on pub snacks. Things could be worse. Led Zeppelin are playing on the jukebox and the bookshelves are stuffed with English literature. Jackie's, as you may have guessed, is a western themed bar. And if we were in any doubt, the clientele would give the game away instantly. We've scarcely seen another foreign face in Yantai but that may be because they've all been hanging out here. Most patrons seem to know the staff and each other. This must be a godsend for any Big Nose who finds themselves posted here on business. Likewise for any tourists who are too lily-livered to try the local grub in case it upsets their delicate little tummies.

The menu implicitly defines 'western' as everything-except-Asian. It's not just American meatloaf or Yorkshire pudding, it's all of that plus Italian, Mexican, French and the rest. Large letters stuck to the glass-fronted kitchen read 'No MSG'. At Jackie's, they know their expat market.

Girlfriend and I discuss whether we could live in Yantai and, for a brief few minutes, the potent Belgian brew facilitates an entirely self-delusional consideration of the pros and cons of life in Shandong Province's lesser cities. 'It's exciting and affordable and by the sea and modernising ...' This from a couple who have just taken a taxi to the only western restaurant in town, rather than sample any of the hundred local eateries.

While we've been kidding ourselves about how we might adjust to Yantai, a downcast young gent has pulled up a stool next to me and ordered a Stella. He's Alex and he's here on business but seems reticent to divulge any further details, despite our prying. The best we can get out of him is that he's 'involved in healthcare', but he's not a doctor. My money is on the pharmaceutical industry, but it's a bet that's never settled.

Alex describes himself as 'ABC' when asked where he hails from. This little acronym, he explains with considerable shock at our ignorance, stands for American Born Chinese. Everyone knows that, apparently.

We deduce that this isn't his first drink of the evening when he goes on a spirited rant about HIV in China. Alex is Californian by birth, accent and manner, but his parents are from the Henan Province, Shandong's south westerly neighbour. He has just come from there and seems intent on telling his tale. We just happened to be the nearest people to his bar stool. Alex is the worst company imaginable but tells a shocking story that often goes untold.

Having been slow to get a foothold in China, the HIV virus is currently having a field day – the UN reckons there will be at least 10 million cases by 2010. Health statistics in China are notoriously unreliable, not least because it is left to corrupt officials in far flung corners of the country to tally up the numbers. International agencies estimate that there are about 300,000 people infected with HIV in Henan Province alone, which Alex insists is the product of local government incompetence. We ask what he means, and then sit back in stunned silence as he goes off on a roll.

The spread of HIV in Henan has gone against the normal trend seen in just about every other country. Typically, the disease finds victims in rundown city slums, spreading among drug users and sex workers, before making the breakthrough into the wider population of the city. From there, migrant workers take it home to the countryside on weekends.

In Henan, Alex fumes, HIV found its way into small villages in the early 1990s, probably via truckers bringing in goods from Laos and Burma. Tragically, this coincided with a catastrophic decision by the Department of Health in Henan to raise extra revenue by selling blood products to pharmaceutical companies.

Ordinary farmers would regularly deposit a pint or so of blood in exchange for around 50 kuai. This was described as a voluntary act but the financial incentive made for an offer too good to refuse. The donations were pooled and the valuable plasma was extracted, before the commercially useless red blood cells were returned to donors.

By the late 1990s, farmers began presenting at clinics with symptoms of what local papers called 'a strange illness'. Over the last decade, large numbers of rural farmers have started to die. And they are still dying. Now, there are hundreds of 'AIDS villages' spread across China and more than sixty per cent of people in some of these forsaken towns are infected.

Of all places, Henan was amongst the worst possible places for an outbreak. It is situated at the intersection of two major transport routes running from north to south and from east to west. All it took was for a handful of people to become infected and the blood scandal saw to it that the disease was distributed throughout the most vulnerable group in the province. And from there, the stream of migrant workers descending on urban hotspots ensured that millions were infected.

Alex says ignorance is the biggest problem. In the beginning, local officials buried the story and buried their heads until 2004 when the central government in Beijing began taking the matter seriously. On World AIDS Day in December 2007, President Hu Jintao was pictured on the front of the *China Daily* newspaper shaking the hand of an AIDS victim, whose face was obscured, in an effort to smash the stigma associated with the disease.

The establishment was not always so progressive. In the 1980s, there had been a very small number of HIV cases amongst Chinese people who had had contact with foreigners. The communist government went so far as to warn against having sex with outsiders and AIDS became known as 'the loving capitalism disease'.

Recent times have seen greater openness to discussing the problem and the government has tightened up the regulation of blood donation clinics. It has also pledged free care for AIDS sufferers and educational grants for AIDS orphans. They are, at least, saying the right things. But it is questionable whether this message is being heard in the remote areas worst affected by the disease.

A survey in 2003 found that seventeen per cent of Chinese citizens had never heard of AIDS, and seventy-seven per cent did not know that HIV transmission could be prevented by using condoms.

I'm reminded at this point that I had to get a syphilis and HIV test as part of the working visa application. Turning up at a clinic with your girlfriend asking for 'two HIV tests, please' is a great way to get patients in a waiting room to look up from their out-of-date magazines.

Just before Alex or we are reduced to tears at the sobering plight of people in AIDS villages, a table is vacated upstairs and we are summoned. How do you pull away from a barroom story that ended with millions of people dying? Fortunately, Alex snaps out of his suicidal stare to proffer a chirpy, 'Well, it was really cool to meet you guys'. I couldn't agree less but wish him well all the same.

A little unsettled, we proceed to order Mexican fajitas with New Zealand beef and succulent chicken breast, which are out-standing by any standard. Just to prove this isn't remotely like a Chinese restaurant, Jackie's serves decent cheese cake and ice-cream, and then charges three times the price of a typical dinner. Worth every jiao.

We'll have to try some indigenous cuisine at our next port of call, which is – where's that map? – Weihai. 'Never heard of it. Let's go.' This is the extent of the planning we put into our travels: looking askance at a map while sipping on coffees at the end of a meal.

Another cheap taxi deposits us on the steps of our hotel where a group of three sweaty, suited businessmen from the Indian sub-continent are being enticed downstairs for a massage. One of them looks particularly reluctant but disappears in pursuit of the porn star masseuse all the same. I hope she uses protective lotions.

Globalisation means the spread of more than just ideas and capital.

17

Colonel Sanders, You Genius

They're selling ice to Eskimos in Weihai. Or something like it. In this forward-looking port city, the fast-food artists formerly known as Kentucky Fried Chicken are flogging spicy fried dinners to the Chinese.

On a prime corner in central Weihai, modish young couples flock to KFC where they can gaze into one another's eyes over a Variety Big Box Meal. The place is packed. The length and breadth of China, KFCs have been popping up on high street corners at a breathtaking rate – a new outlet opens every day. The first helping of finger lickin' good chicken was served to Chinese customers in 1987 but there are now well over 2,000 KFC restaurants and counting. From some points in China – Beijing Railway Station, for example – you can see more than one red shop front with Colonel Sanders' iconic black and white portrait smiling down benignly. Here, he is the personification of globalisation, even giving Ronald McDonald a pummelling.

I haven't been to a KFC since a greasy experience near Old Trafford a few years back when hunger got the better of me, and I'm not about to change that any time soon. But you have to hand it to them. It takes true marketing genius to sell 'American' fast food to the Chinese who can stir fry chicken every bit as swiftly (and cheaply) as the Colonel's foot soldiers can fill their buckets with breaded drumsticks. In China, KFC also serves up traditional Peking chicken rolls, but you get the impression that they could serve steaming cow pats and there'd still be a queue. It's an index of China's lust for foreign brands and their belief that all things foreign must be good.

Weihai is a city on the up. They have invested in aesthetically pleasing street lights and monuments which go beyond the functional. The pavements are well-maintained, the boardwalk is most agreeable and, compared with Beijing, the air is alpine fresh.

The people here have money in their pockets and if they don't already live in new apartment blocks, they will as soon as construction is finished. It can be hard to tell who is poor in China, apart from those few who are obviously starving and homeless. Most appear reasonably well dressed, by western standards. Then again, apart from my Bangladesh boxers and Indonesian Asics, I'm dressed head to toe in Chinese garb. I suppose people here probably get first dibs on cheap polo shirts before they are shipped to Gap warehouses.

Our play-it-by-ear planning forces us to spend our first night in the budget-busting Weihai International Financial Hotel, where scores of staff are buzzing around erecting glossy signage for tomorrow's 'Wealth Management Expo'. How many communists does it take to organise a wealth management expo?

The great thing about soulless overpriced business hotels is the TV. Having been limited to CCTV9 for months, I get a mild dose of the shakes when I discover we have HBO as well as CNN. The satellite picture is black and white, often pixelated and sometimes completely blank, but it's comforting all the same.

At home, the prospect of watching CNN's international business news followed by its golf-centred sports show would be as appealing as a long weekend in Kabul. But here, I'm less fussy.

Having endured the same stories on loop for an hour, we wander into town in search of a Korean restaurant which was recommended by our guidebook. The trouble is that China changes too quickly for any such advice to be worth following, and our target destination has vanished – or, at any rate, turned into a karaoke bar.

Undeterred, we march into a Mongolian barbeque where, with a great deal of assistance from the staff, we figure out how to eat like a Mongol. A large pot of boiling broth is plonked onto a red-hot gas ring in the centre of our table where it bubbles away furiously. We have ordered thinly-sliced lamb, cabbage, mushroom, bean curd, potato and yams, all of which arrive raw. We look curiously at it for a while, eventually accepting that we should just throw it all into the pot and hope for the best.

Apart from having to cook it ourselves, it was among the best meals we've had in China. Too bad I had slurped down half a pint of the spicy soup before a waitress informed me that the water is really just for cooking. She looked a little alarmed to see me drink it so deliberately, but not as alarmed as I was when my intestines began reacting offensively to what turns out to be non-potable water.

Compounding my discomfort is a sign hanging in the gents' which reads: 'Forbid the Bowels'. This, I'm presuming, is Chinglish for, 'Please don't put solid faecal matter in our poorly-plumbed poo pot'. I read the sign from a seated position when the situation is already irretrievable. Naturally, I do what any decent human being would do and leg it before they come after me with a plunger.

Hell is Korean tour groups: megaphones, matching caps, two cameras each and disobedient children.

I'm on a ferry with not one, but three separate gangs of Korean tourists, all of whom are led by prissy girls with 1980s shoulder pads and a loudspeaker they are contractually obliged to use even when speaking to people five feet away. If I could throw just one of them overboard it would dampen the din.

We are bound for Liugong Island twenty minutes from the Weihai wharf. At the turn of the twentieth century, the British occupied the island and there are plenty of jolly old colonial residences still standing. It is also remembered by the Chinese as the founding site of China's first modern navy.

However, for the Japanese, the island holds memories of a resounding victory during the first Sino-Japanese War. Japan's relatively modest armada thrashed China's entire fleet in 1895, despite the Chinese being better equipped and having the supposed benefit of German engineering expertise. This was rather embarrassing, so the island's Sino-Japanese War museum breezes through the more humiliating aspects and focuses instead on what an evil gang of bastards the Japanese are.

The Sino-Japanese War was a disaster for China, stripping it of resources as well as national pride, and ultimately triggering the slow collapse of the Qing Dynasty. Having undergone a period of modernisation in the late 1800s, Japan's development was well ahead of its Asian neighbours and they sought to turn this advantage into influence by seizing treasure, power and esteem from Korea and China. The underlying narrative of the museum is that the Japanese were bullies and the Chinese were brave but dreadfully unlucky heroes. It's scarcely alluded to here, but China's army at the time was rife with corruption, and morale was on the floor: officers were embezzling defence funds and soldiers were indulging in cheap opium.

Once the Japanese had defeated this ragtag bunch of crooked dope fiends, they forced the Qing Dynasty to pay 340,000,000 taels of silver in 'reparations'. This equated to six times the annual revenue of the Japanese state and a whopping twenty-five times as much as the entire war effort cost. A good investment for Japan – if you can ignore all the needless loss of life.

The museum spends more than enough time detailing how Japanese soldiers bayoneted babies and piled bodies up like a mountain of rotting flesh. They (allegedly) kept a handful of locals alive to clean up the mess and then executed them once their work was done. Between this and several other massacres (notably the Rape of Nanjing in the late 1930s) the Chinese are not overly keen on Japan.

I'm beginning to see where Li Jiang, my Japan-loathing student, was coming from with his innate hatred for their neighbour, but maybe I've just bought into the propaganda.

Weihai entertains us adequately for another couple of nights before we move on to Penglai. The haphazardness of our planning is coming back to haunt us again. To get to Penglai, we must pass through Yantai, a city we left just seventy-two hours ago. All of this is north of Qingdao so our trail will have criss-crossed itself numerous times before we leave Shandong Province. It's a little frustrating but we watch a couple of Jackie Chan films on the bus and before long we are in a new town.

At the bus station, ten people vie to sell us useless maps written entirely in *Hanzi,* and another ten peddlers offer us a lift in their pedicabs. It's a familiar and exhausting scene. We refuse all comers while attempting to get our bearings. We have a booking at the Penglai Pavillion Hotel and if these grabby hucksters would unhand me I might have half a chance of figuring out which direction to walk.

One of the small crowd sprints off in a serious hurry. As usual, I wonder irrationally whether he'll return brandishing a machete and demanding my iPod. Instead, he returns with an unlikely accomplice in tow. She's a middle-aged woman with half-moon rimmed spectacles and plum-dyed hair and is running in our direction with supreme inefficiency. The crowd parts to allow her direct access to us. 'Hotel? Taxi?' she says. 'Good price. Do you speaking English? I can find you hotel.'

'Ah, that's the scam,' I mutter smugly to myself. 'She'll whisk us away to her out-of-town B&B and charge us an arm and a leg for the trouble. You won't get me with that old chestnut missus.'

We tell her we already have a hotel booking and we're doing perfectly fine by ourselves, thank you very much – which is entirely untrue. Despite my wariness, she manages to coax us into her taxi, on the understanding that she can help us find the Penglai Pavillion Hotel. I'm certain that we will, at the very least, be charged over the odds.

I smartly ask why the meter is not running, to which she politely answers that it will come on as soon as we start moving. The hotel turns out to be close by and we take the most direct route. She helps us free our rucksacks from the boot of her car and I thank her by rolling my eyes and saying, 'Right – how much is *this* going to cost me?'

'Seven kuai. You're welcome. Nice day.'

Seventy cent? What a crap scam! She must be new to con artistry.

Sooner or later I'll learn that Chinese people are just exceptionally decent and worthy of my trust. But that's probably what they want you to be thinking while they nick your MP3 player.

The hotel was designed by somebody with a passion for wood panelling and is run by a man unconcerned by the smell of urine. The lobby may stink and the rooms are mangy but this remains a four star hotel – it says so on the wall. It seems hotels can pick a number of stars between one and five and have a plaque made to reflect their choice. Four is as good a number as any I suppose.

We're the biggest attraction in Penglai this afternoon. Most people come here for the sun, the seaside and the historic cliff-top Pavillion, but all eyes are on the pair of pasty Irish heads as they canvass another of Shandong's cities. Youngsters impress their parents by shouting 'Hallo' as we walk by. Parents point us out to their kids in the interest of education. A young girl stares at us as we pass, her jaw hanging loose while she taps her sister on the shoulder urging her to look at us. The sister is distracted by the array of weird sea creatures in buckets outside a shop, so the gawker grabs her sibling by the shoulders and turns her in our direction. We're an opportunity not to be missed.

Penglai is essentially a long beach which makes a 'T' with the main street running north to south. The skyline is significantly lower than that of Weihai, Yantai or Qingdao and it has a sleepier feel, despite the busloads of Korean tourists who have made the relatively short trip across the Yellow Sea.

The dining options are limited to freshly caught shellfish, a light-filled noodle bar and, of course, a KFC. Who told the Colonel about this place?

The fish, crabs and clams can be inspected in basins sitting outside the countless undersubscribed family restaurants dotted along the main street by the sea, but we go for something even fresher.

On the beach, a bunch of teenage lads take a time-out from killing each other in a half-joking game of wrestling to offer an exuberant 'Hi'. They are staffing a makeshift beach restaurant which consists of a small gazebo, a barbeque grill, a stove and buckets of shellfish. We'd like to order but the excitable teenagers are hiding behind one another for fear of being on the receiving end of an English oral exam. An older girl, perhaps twenty years of age, appears and takes charge while giddy adolescent boys look on over her shoulder. With a few words of Chinese, a couple of hand signals and a little pointing, we order two crabs. The hostess, with her scraggy, voluminous hair and surfer-dude Bermuda shorts, throws several handfuls of shells into a bucket and tells us it would be 20 kuai for the lot. Deal. Would we like beers? Certainly. The Qingdao brand is 10 kuai but the local stuff is 5 kuai. Two bottles of local it is then.

All this was conducted without a word of English. Fiercely impressed with ourselves, we take seats on the white, plastic patio furniture which is sinking in the sand. It's breezy and the tide is coming in. On one side of the bay is a beautifully lit pagoda at the end of a pier. The other side hosts Penglai's main attraction – the Pavillion.

The crabs arrive. Right, how do you eat a crab with chopsticks? The assembled staff, retired from wrestling, watch in anticipation. We turn to them and give a gormless 'I dunno where to start' grin. They delight in the chance to huddle around our table and show us how to dissect the crab; which bits to eat and which to discard. They do the same with the shellfish. They are not shy about mauling our food and we were surprisingly cool with that. It's deliciously unadulterated by salt, spices and MSG. It might also be the first meal we've eaten all year that isn't swimming in oil.

We may still need occasional binges in western restaurants to keep us sane, but there are sustained signs of progress in our lapsing attitude to food safety standards.

The beers are polished off in a hurry as a wave washes in without warning, helping the legs of our chairs sink further into the sand. We bid our hosts adieu and ramble around the resort until there's no shame in going to bed. It's only about 9.45 pm, but there's not a whole lot to do in Penglai by night.

I've always been fond of Bob Dylan's line, 'I could stay with you forever, and never realise the time'. That's how I feel about Girlfriend ninety-nine per cent of the time. All the same, any sane individuals would lose their marbles while travelling in pairs if they didn't take brief time-outs every few days. She seems equally delighted by my suggestion that I undertake a solo laundrette-finding mission. (Granted, it's not the most mouth-watering prospect, but it was the best I could come up with.)

Living out of a rucksack is no way to run your life. Your clothes take on a musty odour; you *accidentally* wear the same boxer shorts three days running and anything you choose to look for is invariably buried at the bottom of the bag. Every scrap of clothing we brought is in dire need of a spin.

We had passed a laundrette yesterday, just off the main street, but I find it closed this morning. I stare at the sign on the door for a while, but that helps not at all. I could return to the hotel, a failure, but having gone to the trouble of looking up the words for 'wash' and 'dry', it seems wasteful to accept defeat too quickly.

There's a balding man in a filthy vest lapping up the sunshine outside the restaurant next door. Judging by the state of his clothes, it seems unlikely that he's on good terms with his neighbouring washerwoman. I ask whether this is a laundrette and he confirms that it is, turning on his heel and putting a mobile phone to his ear. He spits, then spins back and starts waving his finger at me while trying to read his watch. If he kept his finger still he'd see it was about 10.00 am. Guessing that the laundry lady was on the other end of the phone, I follow him into his empty establishment with my dirty clothing swinging over my shoulder.

He gestures to order that I pop the bag on the table and he begins taking out its contents. Before I know it, my smelly socks and jocks are being thrown around a restaurant. It doesn't much matter what way they land when they hit the table, they've all been worn inside and out. We are joined by a hanger-on, who may or may not be a member of staff. He assists in separating the darks from the whites and putting them into bundles on tables two and three. If a potential diner sticks their head in for a peek at the menu or to assess the ambience, they may think twice before ordering the pork dumplings.

Taking instructions by phone, the restaurateur hands me a ticket and promises the whole lot will be done by this time tomorrow. Just as well, every stitch I own is strewn across his diner (I'm even going commando) and we're catching a train in twenty-seven hours for our final destination in Shandong. But first, there's some serious sight-seeing to attend to.

The Penglai Pavillion is an old fortress precariously situated at the top of a steep cliff overlooking the sea. It was built in 1061 and is packed with temples and shrines and steeped in mythology. It ought to be a site for serene reflection but the Koreans have invaded here, too, armed with their megaphones.

If you ever have the misfortune to get lost in your thoughts in an enclosed space while staring at an eight foot statue of the Eight Immortals, only to find yourself cornered by a shrieking banshee with an amplifier, I'd think no less of you for throwing punches until you are let out. The piercing sound reverberates around the old temple as the guide translates the story for her visor-clad followers. I swear I was about to become one with the Tao when this bitch walked in.

The legend of the Eight Immortals of Penglai is well known across China and has inspired literature and art since the twelfth century, if not before. These characters got drunk one night and decided to cross the sea. However, depending on which version you prefer, they chose not to take a boat like a mere mortal might, and instead used their assorted special powers to traverse the inhospitable waters. They weren't the first gang of lads to think they were immortal after a rake of pints and they won't be the last. It's a legend that sounds like the embellished story of a stag night in Holyhead.

Once inside the ageing walls of the open-plan Pavillion, everything is given a magical air. A tour group surrounds a tree in one of the many beautiful courtyards inside the fort. I edge some weak-looking children out of my way so I can read the plaque on the wall which explains what's so special about this fairly ordinary looking tree. Mysteriously, it states, this 'unique' tree blossoms about a month after other trees in the Pavillion and, in addition, it keeps its leaves a little later than most. This suggests, I conclude, without further help from the signage, that this tree must be a different species of tree to all the others. Still, if they want to call it a miracle, who am I to rain on their charade.

We exhaustively tour the many temples, declining the pitch from salesmen dressed as monks who want us to buy enormous sticks of incense for 300 kuai. After a draining couple of hours, we leave the overrun compound and walk under an arch, opening onto a breathtakingly steep mountainside, which makes me a little nauseous.

A chair lift takes you over the sea to the other side of the valley. It's a long, long way down – which is fine by me because people use this cable car all the time and everything is probably fine. Right? And anyway, we had bought tickets before seeing the size of the drop and I'm not prepared to waste 20 kuai just because I have an irrational fear of the whole contraption collapsing. It won't collapse, but if it did, the fall is certainly not survivable given the unforgiving jagged rocks protruding from the shallow waters below.

Red paint is peeling away from the steel-framed, open-fronted box which might make one question maintenance standards. I get in, banging my head as I do so. A bad start, but hopefully that's my bit of bad luck out of the way, touch wood. Shit, there's no wood. Luckily, I don't believe in all that superstitious mumbo jumbo. I bless myself on the sly.

'Hallo!' shouts an energetic kid in the carriage in front. I unclench the vice-like grip I had on the side bar and give him a dishonestly upbeat wave. That was a big mistake. The four-year-old gets a real buzz out of waving at Big Noses. He starts jumping up on his seat, shaking his carriage and mine.

'Give it over you little monkey,' I say through gritted teeth while trying to hold my smile. Jesus, he's really jumping now. Hyperactive little imp. Did somebody give him Coke this morning? You know it makes him reckless.

He's still bouncing. I can see the headlines: '40 Perish in Peng-lai Plunge'. But who'd know? Nobody has ever heard of the place and the Chinese government think every day is a good day to bury bad news. They'll tell my family I jumped and write a badly trans-lated suicide note to corroborate the story.

He's hopping up and down like a yoyo. I keep smiling and sweating. Will somebody chastise that child before he kills us all? The journey takes five minutes but it feels like a fortnight.

We're over land again but the odds of survival are still 50:50. Oh, he's stopped jumping now, now that it's almost safe.

We make it to the other side of the valley and I leap out of the car, struggling to appear unflustered, and with a new-found ap-preciation for life. We treat ourselves to ice-cream and begin to walk down the mountainside. I look back over my shoulder to see the little ADHD daredevil slurping an ice-pop. What did he do to earn that? He deserves a lecture on health and safety, and a book on risk aversion strategies, not a reward.

'Bye bye', he roars. I curse under my breath but wave back breezily. 'Zaijian, you little shit.'

We spend an hour or so winding our way down the mountain, the sun warming our backs, and return to the hotel. Going down-hill is tough on the calf muscles but this mountain is a mere mole-hill compared to what's ahead of us. This is just training for the main event.

After another outrageously early night, we drag ourselves out of bed nursing tense muscles, collect our laundry and board a bus back to Yantai. From there, there's just a night train and another bus journey, between us and greatness.

18

Immortality Awaits

7,200 steps. I'm going to pay for the privilege of walking up 7,200 steps. Bonkers though that may seem they are not just any old steps. They are the old steps that run up the side of the venerable Taishan, or Mount Tai. It's one of the five sacred mountains of Taoism and it is said that he who can conquer Taishan will achieve immortality. So it should be worth it.

I'm reading up on the task ahead on a train to the Shandong capital of Jinan. This time, we are enjoying the comfort of a soft sleeper. As authentic as the hard seats are, it's not an experience to be endured more than once.

Our four-bunk compartment features a vase of flowers, which helps differentiate it from the six-bed flowerless hard sleeper compartments in the next carriage. We locate our room and greet an abstemious businessman who is wearing thick glasses and a white shirt as he sits tapping randomly at a laptop. His spine is as straight as an arrow and his comb-over makes him look ten years older than I suspect he is. And I'm not keen on his thin ladylike pop socks. Apart from that I'm sure he's a lovely chap. Our room-mate is not into small talk so smiles and nods are exchanged and Girlfriend and I climb up on the top bunks hoping to sleep our way through the nine-hour trip.

There's ample bedding – too much in fact – but the two pillows are a welcome luxury and I settle down for a snooze. I can scarcely believe the relative comfort, but it beats me why they call them 'sleepers'. My eyes are directly under the bright light that illuminates the cabin and my ear is next to a loudspeaker through which seemingly interminable instructions are barked. An announcer is reeling off the most monotonous string of sounds in a lifeless lilt. He is probably detailing the stations we'll pass en route, but he could just as well be reading the classified football results for the all the emotion he's putting into it.

The lights never dim and the noise never relents. The announcer's drone is replaced by an eclectic musical medley starting with China's answer to the X-Factor, moving through some soothing jazz, and on to choppy Chinese rap – or C-Rap for short. I somehow steal an hour or two of sleep by putting in my headphones and listening to Arcade Fire at full volume. It's quite relaxing, honestly.

As we reach Jinan, I hop down from the bunk, ready to roll. Girlfriend asks why I have two pillows. 'Did everyone not get two?' I reply. 'No,' she says, 'the guy below you didn't even have a duvet.'

A straight-faced sixteen-year-old with immaculate English, calling himself Ben, kindly helps us negotiate the mayhem of Jinan's transport depot, physically putting us onto the bus to Taian. He will later email me to make sure everything worked out alright and to ask me if I thought Chinese people are the friendliest people in the world. I'm beginning to, Ben, I'm beginning to.

Arriving in the spacious lobby of our hotel, we wonder why it has only awarded itself two stars. Surely four is the default? The rooms are also surprisingly acceptable, coming complete with the requisite sachets of genital rub. If they had CNN and provided free slippers they would be in with a shout for five stars, as far as I'm concerned.

The telephone rings: 'Massagey, okay?'. Now *that's* a four star service.

I had written off the compact city of Taian, believing it to be just a cluster of hotels arranged around the foot of the mountain to serve immortal climbers. Overshadowed by the holy hill it may be, but it's a charming town with top notch dumpling restaurants and receptive locals. The traffic is permanently gridlocked in the centre of the city but all the action happens within a square mile of the Dai Temple which serves as Taian's focal point. It's an ideal evening walk but don't expect nightlife or to find so much as an open convenience store after 10.00 pm. The KFC probably opens late.

We take a rain check for the lamb dumplings having been lured into an 'Italian' restaurant by the promise of pizza. The Kro's Nest it ain't. The young staff here are attentive (we're their only customers) and thrilled to speak English, so we haven't the heart to complain that the ham on our pizza is a pink-coloured polymer, the base is plywood salvaged from a recycling plant, and the translucent film of red sauce is akin to the syrup squirted on a Mr Whippy. We can't see the kitchen but I can be certain it's just a cloakroom with a freezer and a toaster oven. The waitress shuffles over, neglecting to lift her feet, in a manner common for Chinese girls wishing to affect a ditsy air.

'Is it very very delicious?'

How do you answer a question like that from such an innocent face? 'Mmmm' was our best effort at being diplomatic without baldly lying.

Utterly unsatisfied, we grab twelve dumplings to-go from the joint next door and retire to our two-star hotel to mentally prepare for the greatest challenge of our lives. Is six bottles of beer good preparation, or do top athletes recommend seven?

I awake with a muzzy head, wondering what the odds are of getting out of this mountain-climbing lark. Nil, judging by the lemme-at-'em glint in my climbing mate's eye.

We cough up 200 kuai for tickets through the First Gate of Heaven and we are off. We're following in the footsteps of every historical Chinese figure worth his salt, from Chairman Mao to Confucius himself. The route is littered with temples and monuments, not to mention celestially named archways. The Archway to Immortality near the peak is about 7.5 uphill kilometres away so I may be tempted to take the cable car from the midway point. Girlfriend is having none of it though. Immortals don't do cable cars, says she.

My failure to learn from the painful mistakes of the past has left me with sunburnt thighs and shoulders. Every year without fail, when we manage to squeeze a day or two of beach lounging into our holiday, I go for broke and apply a bare lick of factor two carrot oil, on the basis that if I'm going to get a tan I'll have to get it quickly. And every year I sizzle.

I lay asleep under the midday sun in Penglai two days ago and my legs now look like bubble wrap. Of course, there's only one thing to do with bubble wrap so I now have its aqueous contents streaming down my calf. Beijing's smog cloud usually protects us from direct sunlight for much of the year but in Taian, where the main industry is tourism, the blue skies allow a scorching sun direct access to my bubbling Irish skin.

We are neither of us veteran hikers. A single bottle of water and a pack of Oreo cookies are all we have thought to pack. This leaves us at the mercy of profit-hungry water vendors along the route. Prices start at a modest two kuai per bottle, but the cost gets steeper with the mountain. By the time we near the halfway mark, we are paying six kuai a go and consuming a bottle every couple of hundred steps.

Old and young Chinese are pacing past us with demoralising frequency. There are grandmothers who look like they do this once a week. They must be immortals. A seventy-year-old woman in a polyester pant suit with block-heeled shoes is labouring a little, but no more than we are. She has been named runner-up in our Most Inappropriate Climbing Attire Competition. The ten-year-old girl in the frilly dress, strappy high heels and plastic tiara takes the rosette.

We must look pathetic. Less than half way there, we already look beaten. Perhaps we are mere mortals. Two girls aged about five and seven strike up a conversation in Chinese. We struggle through the basic introductory sentences but we're not really in the mood. Being stared at is no fun when you look like death. Taking pity on us, they offer small foil wrapped treats which they suggest will help reenergise us. Then they demand that we pose for a photo so they can show their friends. (There must be scores of pictures of us on the mantelpieces of complete strangers.)

Unpeeling the foil wrapper, I'm expecting sugar barley or some such glucose boost but the girls' gift has a dark hue and a gritty consistency. It dissolves on contact with saliva, releasing a burst of savoury beef flavour. It's like eating an Oxo cube when you are expecting a hardboiled sweet. I suppress the gag reflex but have to wait an eternal thirty seconds before the girls are out of sight before I can discretely spit it out. Spitting in public – how rude!

Only moments before our systems shut down, we hit the halfway point and tumble like ragdolls onto a receptive grassy mound. It's at once relieving and deflating: the longer we relax the harder it will be to get back up.

I would have paid any sum for an orange flavoured ice-pop but the weathered man at the Midway Gate to Heaven's rest area only wants one kuai. He could learn a thing or two from the rip-off water mongers. We take a breather for fifteen minutes, allowing our legs to partially seize up and then we're off again.

Walking past the cable car is agonising. Lactic acid builds in our muscles, forcing rest stops on us every twenty metres. No sooner have we resumed walking than another pit stop is required. The endless series of stone steps gets steeper and steeper and we've both got new blisters to pop. We blow a fortune on over-priced bottled water but we care not for material things anymore. By the end of the afternoon we'll either be dead or immortal.

A full seven hours after we set out, the summit is in sight. At this point the incline is at its cruellest and it's another half hour before we make it to the top. But we make it! How does it feel to be immortal? Shite, to be honest.

At the tourist information centre next to Taian Railway Station we had reserved a room at one of the mountaintop hotels. Given the choice between a 'low and high standard', we wisely reasoned that a little comfort would be in order. However, Taishan hotels outdo anything you can find at sea level when it comes to offering cruddy accommodation at four-star prices.

We are desperate for a lie down, even though it's just gone 5.00 pm, but there is no way in hell we are resting our heads on these grimy, damp pillows. There are stains on the walls and the thin vertical rectangular window provides only a sliver of light. The window is nailed shut so there's no hope of letting out the musty staleness that permeates the room.

Aching, exhausted, grumpy, we do something we never do – complain. Following a shocking display of shoulder shrugging and calls to the Tourist Office, we are eventually moved to a brighter room which is missing a window. There are freaky insects doing the backstroke around the blocked-up shower plughole, sellotape keeps the bedside locker together, the carpet is threadbare and there is no bulb in the main light. '*That's* more like it,' we say slamming the door. It was a moral victory.

The bedside lamps, by the way, are wrapped in plastic and have large stickers on them which read: 'Warning: Remove plastic before using lamp. Made in China.'

After a celebratory evening meal which consists of 'fried vege-table' (deep-fried battered leaves), 'nut salad' (two dozen salted peanuts in cold water), and 'spicy red bean with beef' (fried green beans encrusted with lumps of animal fat), we make a face at the manager and hit the hay.

Probably as revenge for our failure to take the filthy room and rubbish food in good spirits, reception has kindly provided us with a 'free' wake-up call at 4.30 am. I awake to absolute darkness – the kind that cannot truly be found in urban areas anymore – with no idea who I am, where I am, or why I'm there. My body and mind are in shock. It's not much comfort to realise you're at the top of a Chinese mountain in a horrible hotel, that your muscles have petrified because you have recently climbed 7,200 steps, and there's somebody hammering on your door despite it being 4.35 am.

Every morning, all patrons are awoken to watch the sunrise from a lookout point on the peak. Harnessing every last ounce of available energy, we slide out of bed without bending our limbs and limp downstairs.

This is a once-in-a-lifetime opportunity, says the sign in the lobby. They probably just mean you wouldn't want to do it twice. My complaints are temporarily diverted by the exciting realisation that mildewed winter army coats are being distributed in exchange for a small deposit. These are the real deal: full-length, padded green jackets with fur collars and gold-coloured buttons. We march in single file like a troupe of Red Guard veterans who enjoy re-enacting the Long March before breakfast.

It's dreamlike. I'm standing in a cloud on top of a cliff surrounded by chatter that I can't quite comprehend while looking at my dear girlfriend wearing a Chinese army coat.

We wait patiently for the sun to show itself. Twenty minutes later, half my platoon is abandoning the mission and the other half are locked in debate over whether to follow suit or stay the course. It has quite literally dawned on us that the sun is up and all is now bright. It's 5.25 am. The clouds have deprived us of the once-in-a-lifetime spectacle.

We trudge back to the malodorous hotel room with wet disappointed heads. Grumble, mutter, grumble. This is no way to treat an immortal.

There's nothing in the Rules Governing the Acquisition of Immortality that prohibits the taking of cable cars back down the mountain, so we whizz down to the half-way point in a modern, safe spacepod and take a death-defying bockedy bus round fifty blind bends to the foot of the mountain.

Blocking out the memory of the hotel, the elation of reaching the peak and the arresting view from the top put Taishan on a par with the Great Wall. But, just like our trek to the Wall, it has left us feeling in need of R&R. Beautiful though they are, we've seen all there is to see of Shandong's cities. It's time for something altogether snazzier. It's time for Shanghai.

19

Sleepless in Shanghai

Nobody gives a fiddler's about us in Shanghai. I find myself trying to catch people's eye; offering knowing smiles to strangers thinking they might be half impressed by the sight of my nose. Not a bit of it. This is a truly international city.

Walking along the Bund, Shanghai's quayside strip, it looks as though somebody has stolen a bunch of buildings from a European city and coloured them all in with a HB pencil. Grand old headquarters for banks, newspapers and consulates line the mile-long strip of Zhongshan Road which runs parallel to the city's Huangpu River. It looks decidedly un-Chinese primarily because this is the heart of Shanghai's former international settlement. Change has been a constant in this city's history as control of various quarters was passed around between Japan, Russia, the US, Britain and France. As if that wasn't enough, Shanghai has almost sixty sister cities including the great metropolises of Paris, London, San Francisco, Milan, Osaka and Cork.

The mixture of cultural influences has combined to forge a city full of contradictions and curiosities. This town may house the founding site of the Communist Party (which you can pay into) but it remains a thriving commercial and consumer hub. Whereas Beijing is the modern Chinese capital, Shanghai is an unbridled global trading centre that has grown beyond the boundaries of communism.

The Bund is full of rich-looking Europeans being pestered by persistent salesmen on rollerblades pushing gimmicky electronic toys and a selection of cheap watches. We escape the crowds first by nosing around a couple of the high-ceilinged air-conditioned banks, complete with splendid marble pillars and solid wood furnishings. Once several security guards have encouraged us on our way, we splash out on a Huangpu River boat tour. On the opposite side of the river, across from the Bund, we can see Pudong, in all its glitz. This was farmland until 1990 when the government liberalised financial rules and declared it a Special Economic Zone. Now it's unrecognisable to its former self. New skyscrapers continue to spring up annually and the area is home to well-heeled business types who can pay the equivalent of €10 for a pint of beer in the town's classier establishments. It is a million miles from Shandong. And streets ahead of Beijing.

After an hour cooped up on a boat, we return to the Bund on the west side of the river and make for the adjoining Nanjing Road. This snazzy street was entirely revamped by a French architect in 1998, becoming a busy shopping Mecca. I must confess to finding comfort in the neon warmth of international brand names that line the street, but the incessant badgering by touts selling knock-off DVDs, fake designer shoes and electronic goods is exhausting.

After a whistle-stop tour of the shops, which included a stellar cappuccino at Costa Coffee, it's a brisk ten minute walk to the Shanghai Museum via People's Square.

We slalom through the assemblage of con artists that disguise themselves as students, tour guides and tourists in the well-maintained grounds of the museum. Tiananmen has its share of chancers but Shanghai's tourist traps put Beijing in the ha'penny place. They lounge undercover on park benches, emerge seamlessly from hedgerows and attempt to tag-team you into submission by blocking your alternate routes to the museum.

As in Beijing, they roll out a range of scams from offering you tickets to art exhibitions to tea tasting ceremonies, but it always begins with 'Hello, do you speak English?' Hardened by our past experience, we adopt an air of disgust and pomposity when replying, 'Non! Nous sommes Francais, madame.'

Equipped with floor maps and audio guides, we set off around the impossibly vast Shanghai Museum which is chockfull of excellently preserved artefacts that undoes my impression that Chinese museum curators are not serious about their heritage. Granted, I was basing that assessment on low-grade displays in the tiny museums of anonymous cities. Here, they wouldn't dream of using plaster to fill in gaps in bronze bowls or reconstructing dishes from fragments of pottery surviving from the Qing dynasty.

I won't bore you with the whole multi-storey museum experience other than to say that the bronze exhibition is fascinating, especially the explanation of how casting was done; the furniture display is a little disappointing; the clothes and masks from minority cultures are beautiful and frightening by design; the endless supply of Ming and Qing vases is impressive but exhausting; and I will never see the attraction of garish green jade no matter how well presented it is.

I might add that, as good as the clothing exhibition is, some of the glass-ensconced exhibits are labelled 'Late 20th Century', which seems awfully recent. By that standard, my first school uniform would pass as an exhibit given that it's from 1984. Are the Celts recognised as an ethnic minority in China?

With our minds on minority cultures and our stomachs suggesting it's dinner time, we leave the museums behind and visit the old French Concession where we are welcomed into the Pamir Restaurant by its amiable Uighur owner.

This district looks like it belongs in a separate city to the business and tourist centres near the river. It is full of art deco architecture and tree-lined streets. The Pudong area may have nouveau glamour on its side, but the French Concession, predictably, has a touch of old world class. However, its charm is not altogether Gallic.

I had expected at least a few French brasseries but the dining options are an international stew. Chinese, Japanese, Spanish, Indian and Thai restaurants are all found in what was once dubbed the Paris of the East. In truth, the Concession was always dominated by Chinese locals and even at its most multicultural, the largest group of foreigners hailed from Russia. It's an upmarket neighbourhood but the apartments – new and old – would look foreign to Parisians.

Nor is there anything remotely French about the Uighur grub served at Pamir's, other than the fact that they are serious about good food. The host ushers us up the wooden stairs to the slope-ceilinged loft and pops open a couple of black beers. We begin to order according to our tastes but, apparently, our tastes are just plain wrong, so the owner kindly orders for us. But he does a fine job. Lamb kebabs are mandatory and arrive before we've even completed the order. After that, naan bread, heavy fried noodles, spicy mutton and mixed vegetables sate us absolutely.

The rutted wooden floors and chipped table are rough and ready but we overlook the decor and open another couple of black beers to wash down the last of the kebabs. Scoffing naan bread and lamb skewers under the unsightly ceiling gives the impression of eating in an unconverted attic in Uzbekistan, but the atmosphere is great and this joint is clearly favoured by Shanghai's clued-in expats.

There's a slightly-louder-than-necessary Australian yuppy at the next table talking at two Chinese colleagues. He lays out his whole life story, as if for our benefit as much as anyone else's. He is, perhaps, the quintessential Shanghai Big Nose: He has come here for a few years to make a mint and lives in a fantastically posh apartment near top international schools. His kids, he says, are 'like their mother' and were slow to embrace cultural change but they are getting the hang of things now that they have been here twelve months. He, on the other hand, has adjusted effortlessly. 'I love the way you don't need to learn the lingo,' he adds.

We've no idea whether his friends even speak English because they never get a word in, but it was his story I was most interested in. After less than twenty-four hours, it is already clear that Shanghai would be an infinitely easier city to get by in as a foreigner than Beijing will ever be. The only question is whether we would want it so easy. Living in Yantai would be impractically challenging, but maybe Shanghai just wouldn't be different *enough*. Unless we were here to make money – which wouldn't be a terrible idea – relocating from Dublin to Shanghai would do little to help you understand the Chinese psyche.

I love how quickly I've become a snobbish Beijinger.

Back in our nominally three-star hotel, we discover that Shanghai is a city that never sleeps. Our room is on the third floor facing onto Jiangpu Lu on the north east side of town, which is considerably less swanky than the Bund, Pudong or the French Concession. Ignoring the skyline across the bridge, this lived-in neighbourhood would not look out of place in China's lesser cities. The paths are broken and uneven; the people are either new money or no money; and cranes crowd the sky, above a sea of cement mixers and straining labourers.

As well as luring flush financiers, Shanghai has attracted millions of migrant workers over the past decade, taking its population towards the 20 million mark. Nanjing Street is packed with tourists but the peripheral districts are jammed with workers buzzing around town. Every second mom-and-pop shop dabbles in a little bicycle repair on the side, serving an unyielding demand from low-income locals who need their two-wheelers mended.

There must be 10 million bicycles in Shanghai (somebody call Katie Melua) and they don't disappear after dark. Our attempts to get a solid night's sleep are thwarted by the ceaseless sound of bicycle bells, screeching brakes and rattling suspension. We managed only broken sleep on the night train from Taian last night and are in dire need of eight unconscious hours. But the hum of activity outside is constant. Add to that the fact that the hotel staff think nothing of shouting at one another once the clock strikes 5.00 am, and it's a recipe for sleep-deprived grumpiness.

I'm not sure science museums are ideal for tourists forced into involuntary insomnia, but that's what's on the agenda this morning. Call me a geek, a sap, a goon, a loser, a nerd, a freak, but I love a good science museum.

There are great ones in London, Paris and Chicago (and elsewhere presumably) and the Shanghai Science and Technology Museum looks built to compete with the best. However, it fails to make the grade, in my grouchy opinion.

The big problem for me is that the place is full of children. Some sections are no more than activity centres where kids defy gravity by climbing on the exhibits and aggressively dismantle carefully engineered multimedia touch screens. There are expensive-looking posters on the wall providing bits of background information but these are uniformly ignored by the rampaging hordes of under-twelves.

I don't mind giving over large sections of science museums to school children; I'm all in favour of tricking the next generation into scientific careers so they can get high-end jobs and pay our pensions. But is it too much to ask to have just a few exhibitions aimed at adults? Preferably something you don't have to climb or touch. It doesn't even need to make noise or light up. In hindsight, I probably should have sought out the natural history museum.

It beats me why science gets special treatment when it comes to popularising its knowledge. Imagine a history museum that was solely targeted at nine-year-olds. I do not want museums to be difficult – just interesting to grown-ups.

The larger-than-life-size plastic human body was the biggest disappointment, not just because its funny bits were covered with fig leaves. A narrator lists limbs and organs which light up on cue and the tiny-tot audience say 'oooh' in refrain. A game of 'Operation' would be more instructive. In fact, if it's just a matter of naming body parts, a Heads, Shoulders, Knees and Toes sing-song might at least keep the kids fit.

Some effort at putting information into context is made in the environmental science corner. Here, we can learn how pollution has ravaged industrialised nations: England suffered terrible fog in the 1950s, Lost Angelus is still a smogfest and Japan inflicted countless ecological travesties on itself during its period of development. I circle the exhibit looking for the poster about China's polluted rivers and its permanent urban smog clouds, or at least a warning that China should heed lessons of the past, but no, the purpose here is just to chuckle at the mistakes of Britain, America and, most excitingly, Japan.

Who would have thought science could be so dull?

Unimpressed by the whole experience and still longing for a nap, we skip the IMAX-3D experience and make for yet another museum. Fortunately, the Shanghai Municipal History Museum located in the gaudy Pearl Tower landmark is a treat. Now here's a museum for adults and kids alike.

It's a wander through a full-scale model of 1930s Shanghai streets and shops, delivering an insight into the hedonistic opium-fuelled lives of the ascendency, but also into the hardships faced by working class migrants on whose backs the flashy decadence was built. Too often museums of this kind focus on the lives of aristocrats, perhaps because their life tales are best recorded.

Maybe I'm in a dark mood, but peering back at the misery of the past is as absorbing as knowing what kinds of dressing tables were used in posh people's estates.

Shanghai's story is of political flux. A near constant turnover of foreign concessions unfolds as you walk the mock cobblestones. At one point, there was even a mixed court with local and foreign magistrates to try those who committed crimes in the international zone. This legal experiment was eventually abandoned as it proved tricky to marry the two judicial systems.

The quasi-colonial nature of Shanghai could have bred resentment against foreigners but instead it set the city up as a cosmopolitan bridge between east and west, primed with the flexibility required to embrace globalisation as quickly as anywhere in Asia.

As interesting as the exhibits may be, we are also drawn towards a couple whom we immediately condemn to hell while following discretely. He is pushing fifty, he's fat – nay, obese – balding, jowly, musty and American. There's nothing *wrong* with being American, of course, and his physical attributes are not necessarily of his making either. She, however, is a wafer-thin nineteen-year-old, decked out in $2 shoes, teensy shorts, strappy tops and a bucketload of trashy jewellery. And she too is entitled to dress up for a day at the museum. But you can see where I'm going with this though, right?

He was about to take a picture of a scaled-down model of the Bund when she leapt in front of the camera, desperate to put herself in the picture. This will make it difficult for her sugar daddy to show his holiday snaps to his grown-up kids in Colorado.

She's a joyless type, smiling only when the camera flashes, but she's always by his side whenever he looks like he might want her to be. He explains things to her, reads aloud in a booming baritone, but it is hard to know whether she understands because she never replies. Perhaps she has no English. Perhaps she has no interest. Or perhaps she has been to this museum so many times before with American Johns that it's hard to feign excitement. No matter. He's like a kid with a new toy: all hands, trying to push its buttons to see what it can do, so she must be doing her job. There'll be outrage in Denver when they realise their Sugar Daddies have been outsourced to Asia. Hey, that's globalisation for you.

Leaving the museum and the odd couple behind in the Pudong district, we reckon – or at least one of us reckons – that a bit of shopping is in order so we exhaust ourselves further in a seven-storey shopping mall. It has everything you could want but we quickly agree that we simply cannot afford Shanghai. More importantly, it's a wonder how the ordinary Shanghainese can compete with prices driven skyward by the influx of foreign cash.

Jaded by our day in museums we return to our hotel expecting another sleepless night and we are not disappointed. This place would make you miss the mind-numbing nightlife of Penglai. Or the relative calm of our Beijing apartment for that matter.

Shanghai's 'Old Town' helps us kill time on the final day of our travels. This must be the newest old town I've ever seen, in that it's still under construction. Tourists flock here throwing mad money at pushy vendors looking to offload factory-fresh antiques and mass-produced 'hand-made' silk scarves.

We are irrationally looking forward to the night train home, repressing memories of every other sleepless night train we've taken to date. Whether we sleep or not, it will be comforting to know we're just twelve hours from home. Home is Beijing.

Pained by the Old Town and its new paint smell, we nip down an alleyway into a genuinely aged network of hutongs. People live in relative poverty here. It's a ghetto sealed off from the postcard Shanghai by prohibitive food and clothing prices. We buy four freshly steamed *baozi* for two kuai and feel guilty enough to accept an extra six rather than demand our change in cash. It beats me why people here are so passive in accepting that this is their lot when they quite literally live in the shadow of a towering financial centre. But they are so happy to sell their wares for next to nothing that they throw in a bonus bun for free. I've no idea what we're going to do with eleven *baozi* but I smile, nod and bow manically rather than refuse their generosity.

I'm settling in optimistically for a sleep, clutching my belongings to my chest in keeping with my custom on night trains. We haven't left the station and it's only 8.45 pm but I'm tired enough to nod off immediately. Alas, our temporary roommates arrive and that puts paid to any hopes of rest.

They are aged twenty-one and, wearing the broadest of beaming smiles, they greet us with a loud, 'Hey! How is it going?' Their accents are clipped but have remnants of a Californian twang. However, having never left China, their pronunciation must have been honed while watching *The OC*, *Lost* and *Desperate Housewives*.

We're too tired to humour students keen to practise their English so we endeavour not to engage – but it's not a matter of choice. For these are possibly the worst pair of Chinese students we could have imagined rooming with: These two are on their way to a National English Language Debating Championship in Beijing.

Kevin and Celine are finance and law students respectively. They are brimming with self-confidence and superiority, and seem intent on inflicting their smug monologues on us for the next three and a half hours.

Kevin begins his tiresome performance by treating us to a slideshow of the last debate competition he won (he's a national champ, don't you know) and a trade-by-trade outline of how he has made 160,000 kuai in six months. Basically, he invested in a government-protected steel company and China can't get enough of building materials so he made a 60 per cent profit and is now bloody loaded. Laughing like an Oxford toff, he pronounces, 'Ordinary people want to invest in stocks but they lack an understanding of the fundamentals and fail to appreciate historical trends'. We really like him.

His lecturing style of chit-chat is delivered as though he is addressing a room much larger than this sleeper cabin, and he has a niggling habit of using debate-club language: 'You raise a very interesting point. Allow me to address it in three parts. First, one must consider the role of international legal frameworks in ...' Yawn. I yearn for sleep so badly, like a crack-addict craves a hit.

Celine has her heart set on pursing her postgraduate studies at a US university. Columbia would be ideal but she'd settle for Harvard or Yale. How very reasonable of her. Kevin, by the way, fancies an Ivy League school but has one eye on MIT if the right professor comes a-begging.

Name dropping is the order of the day as Celine reels off the list of clients she deals with at the 'top international law firm' where she is an intern. She works fourteen hours a day as an office skivvy and loves it. If she says Morgan Stanley one more time I'm sleeping in the corridor. I offer them half a dozen stale baozi in a bid to shut them up but they won't take the bait.

Not once did they ask what we do or why we are travelling from Shanghai to Beijing. 'I'm writing a book about all the annoying bastards I meet on Chinese trains,' I might have answered.

The only half-useful piece of information we extract from them is that the mobile phone numbers adorning walls in Yantai, Weihai and certain quarters of Shanghai are contact details for one-stop-shops run by the underworld. If you need a fake passport, a back-alley operation, a loan taken out against your legs, these are the numbers to call.

'What kinds of operations? Kidney transplants? Abortions? Root canals?

'No, no, no, no. Sometimes poor people have a leg removed so they can win pity and beg for money.'

Of course they do. Celine is every bit as charming as Kevin.

Around midnight, with the rest of the carriage successfully sleeping, the teacher from Kevin and Celine's university arrives from next door asking that they pack it in. She apologises meekly in a manner suggesting she has seen the dynamic debating duo inflict similar pain on others in the past. The debaters regard her with indifferent disdain, for she is but a lowly teacher and they are the next generation of Shanghai's elite.

We drift in and out of sleep, longing for our own beds and, in sum, hating Shanghai and its uppity natives. That, apparently, is a prerequisite for true Beijingers. As is often the case, I had to leave Beijing to learn to love it.

20

Peking Man

It's crunch time. We are mid-way through the second semester and the university wants us to sign a contract extension keeping us here for another twelve months. A few months ago, that was out of the question. Now, it's in the balance. We have gotten used to so many irritants: smog, censorship, sweet bread, the language, queue-skippers and being stared at. Not to mention the shockingly routine nature of car crashes.

We witnessed the aftermath of three horrific road smashes today on the way back from visiting the Peking Man site. Drivers enjoy breaking red lights and revving at pedestrians in Beijing city centre, but the traffic gridlock makes it difficult for them to get up enough speed to cause serious catastrophes. Once they get on the ring roads that orbit the city, however, they may race away with unfettered, lane-hopping abandon. Sadly, this resulted in a multi-car pile-up this evening, as well as a side-on collision between a coach and a tank of an Audi, and the overturning of a freight truck. All of this carnage was witnessed on a one-hour trip to the south-westerly outskirts of Beijing where we were promised a prehistoric history lesson.

The remains of Peking Man were discovered in Zhoukoudian by archaeologists in the 1920s. He is somewhere between 250,000 and 400,000 years old and he belongs to an extinct species of human ancestors known as *Homo erectus* – a name which will forever raise a titter in *Homo sapiens'* biology classes.

Our Chinese colleagues who took us to the site had hyped it up royally, to the point where I was half expecting to find a six-foot formaldehyde case holding a perfectly preserved caveman clutching a thick wooden club. Imagine my disappointment then when we arrived to find that Peking Man had been stolen.

The interpretive centre walks you through the story of the excavation, complete with grainy black and white photographs, and there are plenty of casts and replicas of real bones. But the most significant item on display is the pair of large wooden crates, for it was in crates just like these that Peking Man was carefully wrapped for shipping to the US in 1941 for safe keeping. Whoever put the priceless remains into those boxes were the last *Homo Sapiens* known to have seen the fossils.

The prevailing myth – although there are very many – is that the Japanese kidnapped Peking Man, who had been in the hands of US marines, but his whereabouts remains an unsolved mystery. He's about five feet tall with a low, flat skull and a protruding brow. If you see him, tell him he's badly missed at Zhoukoudian.

We have arrived for pizza in Kro's Nest in Beijing's eastern Chaoyang District. The food is still excellent. Purely coincidentally, we bump into Martin and Cheng Cheng who are polishing off some cheese sticks before moving on to The Den to meet workmates. Sounds like a plan, we say, and efficiently enjoy a medium-sized Hawaiian before following them the short distance down the road.

On the way, we see Jonathan, our Canadian co-worker, and his new wife Qu Yi who are en route to Kro's Nest of all places. They'll follow us to The Den where we discover another bunch of our colleagues who have been enjoying the hospitality since lunchtime – judging by the state of them.

Maybe there are only a handful of places popular with expats, but it suddenly feels like everyone I know in Beijing is within a 100 metre radius tonight. I even bump into Greg the Frenchman who I had previously befriended last month while watching a football match in the Rickshaw – another expat haven down the road. Greg is passing time here while he waits for college to start in Switzerland. His father works for Air France so he has spent his childhood all over Asia living the international high life and he's a little down on Beijing. Well, I won't hear a bad word said against the place, so I challenge him to defend his allegations concerning rude locals, dirty streets and dodgy food. Sure, he has a list of concrete examples of all the above but I plead with him to reserve his judgement.

'These are the complaints of a Beijing beginner, Greg, teething problems. Just give it time. How long did you say you'd been here by the way?'

'Eighteen months.'

'Oh, right.'

So Greg wasn't for turning, and others join in the Beijing bashing once he gets the ball rolling.

This is all feeding into our decision-making process. Should we stay or should we go? We're getting conflicting advice and the issue is being clouded by draft Tsingtao.

We flit to the other side of the bar like social butterflies where Martin and his work crew of Beijing veterans impart various shades of advice on how long is too long to stay in China. The consensus is that you are still a newbie after one year but that anything north of five years is bad for your physical and mental wellbeing. The conversation moves on but my increasingly beer-sodden brain is dwelling silently on the big decision. I say little for the rest of the night, while Johnny Logan's 'What's Another Year?' loops around my head.

Standing outside awaiting the sight of a taxi with an illuminated roof sign, Girlfriend remarks on how far we've come, how much we've learned, how we have adapted. She's right, and in the heady haze of a night's binge drinking, I'm suddenly full of it.

'I'm beginning to feel like it would be a shame to move on now, having overcome the tough bit. What are you thinking?' she asks.

'I'll tell you exactly what I'm thinking,' I say, stepping solemnly up onto a discarded beer crate and taking a deep intake of breath. I launch into a rousing speech. Suddenly I'm JFK, Jim Larkin, Robert Emmet and Winston Churchill, albeit with a smaller, less exuberant audience:

'I am the modern day Peking Man – a foreigner willing to understand Beijing as much as wishing to be understood.

When I came here I was a man on a mission, though I knew not what that mission was. It revealed itself to be a journey to the heart of China. But not only that, it was a quest for my own identity. Friends, I am now several steps closer to accomplishing that mission but this cannot be the end.

There is, to paraphrase a lesser orator, a lot done but more to do.

How could I now leave my many new friends who at this moment do slouch half cut in The Den?

How could I now abandon the thin-based pizzas any man would travel half the world to eat?

How could I now trade the West for the East when the latter is a hive of excitement and there's shag-all good going on in the former?

A return to the West would mean a return to office politics and penny-pinching overlords. It would mean high rents, high stress and, given the availability of half-decent desserts, high cholesterol. If change is what we truly seek, then staying the course is the only option.

I have fallen for this city, for its quirks and its contrariness, for its unfocused ambition and functional disorder.

I am a modern citizen of the world, in the world's fastest moving city. I have adjusted to the food, I have learned how to say "no MSG please", I have found bars that show Premiership football and serve draft beer.

I am at home here, and here I must stay.

Friends, drunkards, taxi men – Ich bin ein Beijinger!'

With that, and to the sound of an ironic slow clap, a cyclist throws his head over his shoulder, blindly releasing a throaty spit into the night. It lands directly on my shoulder.

'Ah fuck this – I'm going home.'